THE DISCIPLE OF CHRIST

THE
DISCIPLE
OF CHRIST

Vaughn J. Featherstone

Deseret Book
Salt Lake City, Utah

ISBN 0-87747-910-0
Library of Congress Catalog Card Number 84-71706

Deseret Book Company
P.O. Box 30178
40 East South Temple
Salt Lake City, Utah 84130-0178

Contents

Preface

I would like to pay tribute to my son Scott, who, while serving in the Navajo Indian Mission, was searching for a way to improve. He earnestly studied the scriptures and found what he was looking for in Helaman 3:29:

> Whosoever will may lay hold upon the word of God, which is quick and powerful, which shall divide asunder all the cunning and the snares and the wiles of the devil, and lead *the man of Christ* in a strait and narrow course across that everlasting gulf of misery which is prepared to engulf the wicked. (Italics added.)

He said, "That is it—to become a man of Christ."

Each chapter of this book is devoted to a trait or concern that would lead a person to become a man or woman of Christ. It is my hope and prayer that by incorporating these traits into our lives, each of us will become a true disciple of our Lord.

1

Reverence for the Savior

The Master taught us how to care and love. Said He, "As I have loved you, . . . love one another." (John 13:34.) He also said, "What manner of men ought ye to be? Verily I say unto you, even as I am." (3 Nephi 27:27.) The perfect model in all of eternity gave His life for all of humanity. He counseled us to love as He has loved us. How did He love us?

In the eternal realms of our pre-earth life, our beloved Father in heaven presented a divine plan whereby all of His spirit children could be born into mortality and be tested, tried, and eventually proven. This plan required a sacrificial lamb, one without spot or blemish.

Not one of us had experienced mortality. The unknown always brings concern, doubts, and fears of inadequacy. Our immediate concern was that we would be placed on a telestial sphere far away from God and be tested and tried by the passions and desires of the flesh, which we had never known. We, having been taught the full consequences of mortality and of our failure or success, were undoubtedly told that "strait is the gate and narrow is the way, which leadeth unto life, and few there be that find it." We also must have learned that "wide is the gate, and broad is the way, that leadeth to destruction, and many there be that go in thereat." (Matthew 17:13-14.)

Knowing that a veil of forgetfulness would be placed

between our pre-earth life and mortality, we may have had a tremor of doubt that we might lose our way. Heavenly Father, knowing the beginning from the end, knew that Adam and Eve would fall from His grace through disobedience and that all of the posterity of Adam, including all generations yet unborn, would transgress and fall short of the mark. Therefore, it would be necessary to provide a Savior and a Redeemer to satisfy justice. The appointed one would have to be perfect, flawless, and without blemish, and be willing to offer himself as a sacrifice to atone for the sins of all and to redeem mankind from Adam's fall.

Two responded to Heavenly Father's question "Whom shall I send?" We will discuss only the worthy one, He whose heart was pure, whose commitment was to do His father's will, knowing that failure was possible and that eternity would hang in the balance for all of the myriads of God's other children. Jehovah said, "Here am I, send me." A great hosanna shout must have carried through the eternities. (Abraham 3:27; Job 38:4-7.)

The Father, with absolute confidence and boundless love, gave this assignment to the Firstborn in the spirit world. We should love Jesus because only He could qualify as our Savior and was willing to place Himself on one side of the scale while all of mankind balanced precariously on the other. His absolute trust in His Father and our Father, His faith and courage, His total submission—all give us sufficient reason to love Him.

How has He loved us? All that was designed and planned had to be carried out. The commitment had to be complete and absolute. There could be no turning back.

As the mortal Christ, the hour of His ministry and trial had come. He blessed the sick and healed them. The blind were made to see, the deaf to hear. Adulterers were cleansed, the lame walked, the heavyhearted found peace, the poor found hope, and the widow found comfort. All mankind found hope in the gospel plan.

The Savior's ministry was brief but profoundly consequential. From Bethlehem came the Prince, from Nazareth the Carpenter, from Galilee the Fisherman for all mankind. Try to comprehend the trial of fasting forty days. Consider the many unknown times when He prayed all night. Contemplate the constant demands on His time. "The foxes have holes, and the birds of the air have nests; but the Son of man hath not where to lay his head," He said. (Matthew 8:20.) Always, He was imposed upon. Men lowered a man with the palsy through the roof to receive a healing blessing from Him. He could have been indignant, but He was not. He healed the afflicted one. He fed the hungry by the thousands. He administered to the sick and healed all who came.

The path He trod led eventually to the atonement and redemption, for which He had taken an eternity to prepare. His course was set by God, but He was at the controls and could have abandoned the course even at that final hour.

Praise be to God, He entered Gethsemane's quiet garden. Leaving the disciples behind, He walked where only God could walk. He approached that hour with a loneliness that none can comprehend. He knelt, for the hour had come. That night all of our Father's children waited for the result of this foreordained hour. Our Lord summoned all the powers of His Godhood and His mortal, physical strength with an absolute, uncluttered comprehension of what was yet to come in those few brief moments. He was prepared for that night.

Never before nor since nor ever again will such a monumental moment come. The condemning acts, the most vile transgression, the deepest evil deeds of the repentant sinner began to rest on this spotless One. Like a great deluge they continued to pour upon Him—the weight and immensity of the penalties of all broken laws crying from the dust and from the future—an incomprehensible tidal wave of guilt.

We know not how long this excruciating mental suffering lasted. We know only that so exquisite, so extreme was the trial, that he actually sweat blood.

The hour for which all of humanity had awaited came and passed, and glory be to our God, our dear Lord Jesus Christ met the crucial test and satisfied every demand of justice.

He had been placed on the scale to indemnify us as only He could, being spotless and sinless and without blemish. Heavenly Father's trust and confidence in His Only Begotten Son had proved justified.

What incomparable, magnificent love and eternal pride must have filled the bosom of the Father. Celestial tears must have been shed. A tremor of a grateful parent must have shaken eternity as Jesus met this one agonizing hour and won for all the glorious victory.

Think of the hatred, the utter contempt, the wrath and anger Lucifer must have felt, knowing that the One he despised more than all others in eternity had not wavered.

We may never know how the Savior's act cleansed and satisfied justice for all who would exercise faith, repent, and be baptized. No mortal soul could have physically or spiritually suffered what Jesus did. We would have faded into unconsciousness or given up the ghost. Because Jesus was begotten by God, He had the power within Him to withdraw at any moment. He also had the capacity to endure the ultimate agony without losing consciousness. The degree of suffering could not be partially blocked; it had to reach the exquisite limit for every broken law.

When His hour was past, He claimed the victory. The serpent's head had been crushed. From the Garden to Golgotha's hill was a matter of course. Thousands have been crucified, but only He came to the tree with the power to give His life. It could not be taken from Him. Nonetheless, the eternal episode in Gethsemane had left His physical body consumed almost to the limit. His physical strength was near exhaustion. A cross that He normally could carry with little effort weighed upon Him until it drove Him to His knees. Unlike Gethsemane's experience, the crown of thorns that pierced His skin brought forth drops of blood spontaneously. What was the suffering from the large spikes driven through His trembling flesh compared to His previous supreme mental struggle? He knew that the victory was His.

Now it was only a matter of time. The flesh continued to suffer exquisitely, but His spirit, no longer bowed down with grief, stood erect and tall. The flesh cried out for water, but the spirit had drunk from the Father's fount. But there was one last, great trial.

The Father withdrew His spirit altogether and left His dearly beloved Son to suffer, agonize, and die alone. The Father's spirit had not withdrawn in Gethsemane, and Jesus had called on the additional strength as a necessity. Now He was alone. The angels must have wept. We all weep when we comprehend Golgotha.

What must have seemed an eternity was past. Jesus voluntarily did that which no mortal could have done to Him—He gave His life as a redeeming sacrifice for all mankind. The Son of God was dead. By His own agency the last bitter act was completed. His eternal commission had been completed. Through His atoning sacrifice every soul who had lived or would live would be resurrected.

And the relatively small flock who would exercise faith in Him, repent of their transgressions, and be baptized and then receive all of the other saving ordinances, enduring to the end, would find safe harbor in the eternal realms of God, our Father.

We sing:

> *I stand all amazed at the love Jesus offers me,*
> *Confused at the grace that so fully he proffers me;*
> *I tremble to know that for me he was crucified,*
> *That for me, a sinner, he suffered, he bled and died.*
> —Hymns, *no. 80*

No wonder we build temples, houses of the Lord. No wonder that every prayer to our God is closed in Jesus' holy name. Can anyone question that His opening the door, which only He could enter first, would give entry to all who would follow? Could we possibly be His disciples and not do everything in our power to share the gospel? What unworthy followers we would be, after all that has been done for us, if His work and glory did not also become our work, if we did not become His true disciples. Would any one of us knowingly transgress, with an attitude of repenting later, if we realized our acts were crucifying Him afresh?

Through faith in Christ we find peace and security. Through trust in His grace and mercy we find solutions to every problem. Through Him, we find strength to live and to overcome every obstacle. Our reverence for him should know no bounds.

2
Love for the Words of Christ

For me it would be impossible to have one favorite scripture. Too many verses are too priceless to single out any one of them. To read and ponder such verses can be compared only to the thrill that comes from hearing angelic choirs, or feeling the Holy Ghost carry a message to the heart, or knowing the majesty of the message and rhythm of the true poets. Those who study, ponder, and consume such words of the prophets enlarge their souls and acquire a celestial point of view.

One scripture I can never read without feeling love for the great prophet who wrote it. Always tears bedim my eyes:

> I, Nephi, have written what I have written, and I esteem it as of great worth, and especially unto my people. For I pray continually for them by day, *and mine eyes water my pillow by night,* because of them; and I cry unto my God in faith, and I know that he will hear my cry. (2 Nephi 33:3; italics added.)

And there are many, many other verses I love:

> The Lord spake unto Enoch, and told Enoch all the doings of the children of men; wherefore Enoch knew, and looked upon their wickedness, and their misery, *and wept and stretched forth his arms, and his heart swelled wide as eternity; and his bowels yearned; and all eternity shook.* (Moses 7:41; italics added.)

7

Lo, I have given thee a wise and an understanding heart. (1 Kings 3:12.)

Unto the pure all things are pure. (Titus 1:15.)

Greater love hath no man than this, that a man lay down his life for his friends. (John 15:13.)

Blessed art thou, Nephi, for those things which thou hast done; for I have beheld how thou hast with unwearingness declared the word, which I have given unto thee. (Helaman 10:4.)

If all men had been, and were, and ever would be, like unto Moroni, behold, the very powers of hell would have been shaken forever; yea, the devil would never have power over the hearts of the children of men. (Alma 48:17.)

O that I were an angel, and could have the wish of mine heart, that I might go forth and speak with the trump of God, with a voice to shake the earth, and cry repentance unto every people. (Alma 29:1.)

If men come unto me I will show them their weaknesses. I give unto men weakness that they may be humble; and my grace is sufficient for all men that humble themselves before me; for if they humble themselves before me, and have faith in me, then will I make weak things become strong unto them. (Ether 12:27.)

The Lord said unto me: If they have not charity it mattereth not unto thee, thou hast been faithful; wherefore thy garments shall be made clean. (Ether 12:37.)

Now, after the many testimonies which have been given of him, this is the testimony, last of all, which we give of him: That he lives! For we saw him, even on the right hand of God; and we heard the voice bearing record that he is the Only Begotten of the Father—That by him, and through him, and of him, the worlds are and were created, and the inhabitants thereof are begotten sons and daughters unto God. (D&C 76:22-24.)

He has heard our prayers, and by revelation has confirmed that the long-promised day has come when every faithful, worthy man in the Church may receive his holy priesthood, with power to exercise its divine authority, and enjoy with his loved ones every blessing that flows therefrom, including the blessings of the temple. (D&C Official Declaration—2.)

How can such words be read, studied, and pondered upon and not thrill the soul? It is easy for me to understand how the prophets can be carried away in the Spirit when meditating upon such things. Limited as I am, my soul feels to melt when I read such spiritual eloquence and beauty. I feel as though my heart would burst with goodness and gratitude for my God.

Through His great mercies the Lord seems to give those who truly seek Him an occasional momentary glimpse into the eternities, a glimpse that is not so much seen as felt.

We can discipline our minds to seek out, search, and find great ideals and thoughts to ponder. The greater the search and study, the greater the appetite of this marvelous instrument—the mind—God has given to all of us. To ponder the words of the prophets, to teach the words of the prophets, to sing the words of the prophets, which are the words of Christ, comes as near ecstasy as anything we can wrap our minds around. We obtain the same exquisite sweetness of soul when we read beautiful words as when we perform Christ-like acts of service.

What a waste of the mind of man to let it wander, roam, and think upon things of a lesser level. The mind and heart can be given to uplifting and enobling ideas, to work-a-day activities that are essential to earning a living, or to petty gossip, debasing thoughts, lustful acts, revenge, jealousy, perversions, and all manner of lewd and unworthy considerations.

We are invited by the Lord to search the scriptures. What a thrilling thought! Wouldn't it be a sweet bequest to your children and grandchildren and descendants yet unborn to list in your journal the scriptures that have been your favorites? Share with your posterity the verses that have helped you during the darkest hours you have faced.

As I have written this chapter, a multitude of other scriptures, equally as powerful, equally as beautiful, have flowed through my mind. All of them have their silent, quiet, holy impact.

The Miracle Worker is a movie about Helen Keller. At times during this great portrayal of a teacher trying to communicate with a blind, deaf girl, I wept. The first time was when the teacher, Anne Sullivan, was disciplining (training) Helen and the whole family turned on her. They contended that Anne was cruel and unkind to expect so much from this soul who had never had any more expected from her than from a dumb animal. Helen's elder brother was the only one who could see the vision of what the teacher was doing, and he came to her rescue during her desperate attempts to help Helen.

The second emotional experience came as Helen finally discovered the means of communication with which her teacher had been instructing her a thousand times or more. What a marvelous portrayal of a soul lighting up from the inside. The window to her soul had the shutters and drapes removed, and she could communicate.

The third experience came at the end of the movie when a grateful deaf, blind Helen went to her who had poured light into her soul and, as the only expression of gratitude she knew, kissed her on the cheek. How much more should we show our gratitude for the words of Christ, which open our souls to the light of eternity.

The scriptures, the writings of the prophets, hymns, and poetry expand our souls. At President N. Eldon Tanner's funeral service, the Tabernacle Choir sang "How Gentle God's Commands." I wish I could describe to you what happened inside my soul. I have sung that hymn many, many times. But only this once did I really hear and feel it. For the first time I wept when the choir sang it.

As I have since pondered over the experience, I have determined that a combination of things happened. First, the members of the choir and Jerold Ottley, their conductor, had such great love for President Tanner that their souls were in the music. The fact that President Tanner, this noble, great soul who was a counselor to four prophets, was being eulogized added greatly. But I believe I really, spiritually heard the words and understood them for the first time.

What was this experience like? Imagine that the Tabernacle Choir is singing more beautifully (like a celestial choir, which they were) than you have ever heard them. Imagine that you are in the Tabernacle, which is filled with wonderful Latter-day Saints, and in the presence of the Prophet and all the Brethren. The choir sings these words:

> *How gentle God's commands!*
> *How kind his precepts are!*
> *Come cast your burdens on the Lord*
> *And trust his constant care.*
>
> *Beneath his watchful eye,*
> *His saints securely dwell;*
> *That hand which bears all nature up*
> *Shall guard his children well.*
>
> *Why should this anxious load*
> *Press down your weary mind?*
> *Haste to your Heavenly Father's throne,*
> *And sweet refreshment find.*
>
> *His goodness stands approved,*
> *Unchanged from day to day;*

I'll drop my burden at his feet
And bear a song away.

—Hymns, *no. 67*

Could you feel spiritually what I am trying to share with you? Truly, how gentle are God's commands. How beautiful and kind and sweet His precepts are.

In the few short years I have been a General Authority, many things have changed in my life. Mostly they have intensified. It has been my experience that the Brethren are attempting to live as near the perfect model as possible.

Reading the beautiful words of the prophets as recorded in the scriptures provides a vicarious experience so real and so sure that our witness is just as true as if we had been there. This Church of Jesus Christ of Latter-day Saints is the Lord's church. The Church leaders are God's leaders and will never lead us astray.

Elder Monson once said, "Beautiful souls always have beautiful words to speak." And so it is with our beloved brethren. I love them and I know they are men of God who speak the words of Christ, and that He is at the helm.

3
Courage

When I was only a boy, I used to fantasize about doing some courageous, heroic deed. I could see myself rushing into a blazing building to save a child or diving into a river to help someone who was drowning. I suppose most of us would like to do something that sensational.

Through the years I have discovered that courage has a thousand faces. Many times the most heroic deeds are done in silence, alone, where no eye can see but where courage was nonetheless needed.

Sometime you may wish to look in *Roget's Thesaurus* under the heading *courage*. In addition to hundreds of words that describe or are synonyms for courage, there are several statements about courage that are worthy of consideration: Dorothy Bernard described courage as "fear that has said its prayers." General Patton defined it as "fear holding on a minute longer." Plautus said it is "taking hard knocks like a man when occasion calls." La Rochefoucauld had a slightly different concept of courage, defining it as "doing without witnesses that which we would be capable of doing before everyone."

It is interesting that not one of these definitions includes sensationalism. However, there are other synonyms of courage, such as "serve oneself," "steel oneself," "take heart," "inspirit," "bold as a lion," "resolute," "unafraid," "heroic," "valiant," "run the gauntlet," "go through fire and water," "march up to the cannon's mouth," and "have the courage of one's convictions." This may give us insight as to why it is so essential for the disciple of Christ to be a person of courage.

On September 3, 1975, I received a letter from Jeane Woolfenden, who shared with me an account of an unusual man named David Boone:

> David Boone is thirty-six years old and has been a cerebral palsy spastic all his life. His small, twisted body barely functions, yet he has learned to walk a few steps in a specially built walker. It was through the concern of neighbors that Dave was taught the gospel and baptized. He is now an elder and has his endowments. He goes to the temple monthly. If you could see him, you would realize how dedicated he is to even try.
>
> He is very active in our group. The fellows take turns in bringing him. They throw him over their shoulders like a sack of potatoes and off they go. The specialness of Dave was really shown to me after an accident he was involved in just before the holiday on July 24. That Monday a busload of handicapped people toured Bingham Canyon mine. On the way down the canyon the brakes went out. The bus driver warned the occupants before he rammed some cars to cushion the blow. Dave was sitting next to a girl he likes but who is even more helpless than he. He threw himself across her to protect her. She got a broken toe. He broke both ankles, cracked his back, and cut his face very badly.
>
> That was Monday. He told one of the fellows who went to administer to him to excuse him from family home evening activities that night. He had been calling another fellow at 6:30 every morning to get him up. He missed Tuesday morning but was back on the job Wednesday morning from the hospital bed. He was much more concerned about everyone else than himself.
>
> Our family-home-evening group decided to write him letters to cheer him up. We also visited him, but we wanted to write letters because he can't read and his mother would have to read the letters to him. We wanted her to know of our concern for him, too. While we were

writing, some of the fellows that know him well told us some things about him.

Since the fellows have to carry him wherever he goes, he watches his weight—he is ruthless with himself and won't gain one extra pound. When Dave isn't sitting or being carried, he's lying down, so it's not easy to maintain his weight.

Whenever he goes out he makes sure that there's a way for him to get back early. He doesn't want his parents to worry or wait for him to come home to help him to bed.

He is dedicated to the gospel and to doing missionary work. He does missionary work at the handicapped center and even teaches those of us who have been members for years.

He has an undying good attitude. Once when I visited him he told me that if it became possible to be married during this life, he'd do it. "But," he said, "the millennium will be my day. I'm going to run and jump and read and help others and find a good wife and raise good children. But for now I'm going to do everything I can and do the Lord's will for me, and they aren't going to keep me down as long as I can help it."

He is unashamed of his condition. He is anything but bitter or self-pitying. He is an example to anyone with much less of a problem in life.

David Boone's story may remind even the most fearful or introverted that courage is a state of mind. When word was received by Jim Bowie's mother that her son had died at the Alamo, she calmly replied, "So Jim is dead. I'm sure they didn't find any bullets in his back." During World War II, a textile worker said, "I told my wife I'd already laid down my life before I went overseas and if I came home I'd come home with medals on my chest." President David O. McKay once said that no act is ever committed without first having been justified in the mind. That is a true statement of courage as well as transgression. Our thoughts prepare us for some moment of destiny in the future. We may rise or fall, and our thoughts will govern all.

I have written a poem, "But What of Him?" that speaks of one who lacked the courage to face up to his responsibilities:

With stooping form, his eyes cast down, he waited
   patiently.
His words rang in his listeners' ears, they watched so
   silently.
"Let he who has not sinned be first to cast or throw a
   stone."
His writing finger accused them all, cowering under
   guilt they'd known.
They left, these men, whose inner thoughts he'd read.
"Woman, where are thine accusers?" in sweet accord
   he said.
"There are none, Lord." She wept, contrite tears bedecked
   her face.
"Neither do I condemn thee now, forgiveness cometh as a
   grace."
With humble soul, adoringly, she knelt humbly at his feet.
His precious words had cleansed her soul, his love
   profound and sweet.

Dear Jesus, God of love and Savior of my soul,
Thy redeeming love has saved me; come, please take
   control.
Hers was forgiveness through the Lord, her guilt was swept
   away—
Taken in sin, forgiven by him, a glorious redeeming day.
But what of him who lay with her, whose sin was ne'er
   revealed?
Can redeeming blood wash white his sin, while secretly
   concealed?
She had been dragged by discovering men, while he
   sneaked away.

*She in terror prepared to be stoned, while he escaped that
     day.*
*Why did the men bring only her, to face this great
     disgrace?*
*Were lust and guilt and evil thoughts revealed in every
     face?*

*Did he return to wife and child with a false and lying
     heart?*
*Was adultery's vice less for the man than the woman's
     beguiled part?*
*What craven coward would sneak away and leave her all
     alone*
To suffer death by anxious men prepared to cast a stone?
*Run off and hide and look not back, your soul took
     coward's flight;*
*With swiftest speed, you fled the deed, to hide in deepest
     night.*
*But the Master came, yea, God in Man, to ransom free her
     soul.*
*While your conscience taunts your mind, like waves upon
     a shoal.*
The coward's lie still hidden long will temper you and me.
*No cleansing blood can wash the sin, no power can set
     you free.*

*For life is short, and long the years we live beyond the
     grave.*
In Christ alone can we be free, His atoning blood he gave;
*For those who love and follow Him, the precious price he
     paid.*
And come we will, for come we must, in tears or unafraid.
We'll walk the path of justice, the extracted price so great;
All must come to Gethsemane's time, whether soon or late.

And though you were not caught and slipped quietly
away,
The rod will heal the sin, dear man, in a compensating
way.
To all who share the selfsame sin, and suppose it's hid
from sight,
There is no peace, there is little hope, bitter tears will be
thy plight.

We must have the courage to face up to our responsibilities, no matter how difficult they may be. Winston Churchill said, "We have not journeyed all this way across centuries, across oceans, across mountains, across prairies because we are made of sugar candy." This statement is true, especially of Church members who live their religion. Great winds are blowing toward us—political, satanic, inflationary—crude and ruthless winds that will test us to the limit. We are not made of sugar candy. We have not become soft as a feather pillow. In fact, the reverse is true. We are becoming stronger and more courageous.

There is a marvelous passage in the Doctrine and Covenants that sends chills down my spine:

> Let my army become very great, and let it be sanctified before me, that it may become fair as the sun, and clear as the moon, and that her banners may be terrible unto all nations; that the kingdoms of this world may be constrained to acknowledge that the kingdom of Zion is in very deed the kingdom of our God and his Christ. (D&C 105:31-32.)

We can make a difference. Boyd Ivie, the chief Scout executive of the Great Salt Lake Council told of an experience he had had in Tokyo just after World War II. It was May Day. The Communists were having a giant demonstration. They came to the city square, went to the flagpole, lowered the American flag, threw it on the ground, and desecrated it. They were looking for a match so they could burn it. Boyd Ivie and his flight crew were in the crowd. They came out of the crowd, picked up the American flag, and hoisted it back to the top of the pole. There were thirty other Marines in the crowd, and they came forward, locked arms with the flight crew, and protected the flag for several hours until the demonstrators left.

In addition to all of this, there is a quiet, assured, courage that comes from trust and innocence. Let me share with you another dimension of courage from Dostoyevsky's classic *The Brothers Karamazov.*

Lizaveta was a dwarfish creature, "not five foot within a wee bit." She wandered about, summer and winter alike, barefoot, wearing nothing but a hempen smock. Everyone regarded her as an idiot, so she was especially dear to God. Many in town tried to clothe her better, always rigging her out with high boots and a sheepskin coat for the winter.

> But, although she allowed them to dress her up without resisting, she usually went away, preferably to the cathedral porch, and taking off all that had been given her—kerchief, sheepskin, skirt or boots—she left them there and walked away barefoot in her smock as before. It happened on one occasion that a new governor of the province, making a tour of inspection in our town, saw Lizaveta, and was wounded in his tenderest susceptibilities. And though he was told she was an idiot, he pronounced that for a young woman of twenty to wander about in nothing but a smock was a breach of the proprieties, and must not occur again. But the governor went his way, and Lizaveta was left as she was. At last her father died, which made her even more acceptable in the eyes of the religious persons of the town, as an orphan. In fact, every one seemed to like her; even the boys did not tease her, and the boys of our town, especially the school boys, are a mischievous set. She would walk into strange houses, and no one drove her away. Every one was kind to her and gave her something.

If she were given a copper she would take it, and at once drop it in the alms-jug of the church or prison. If she were given a roll or bun in the market, she would hand it to the first child she met. Sometimes she would stop one of the richest ladies in the town and give it to her, and the lady would be pleased to take it. She herself never tasted anything but black bread and water. If she went into an expensive shop, where there were costly goods or money lying about, no one kept watch on her, for they knew that if she saw thousands of roubles overlooked by them, she would not have touched a farthing. She scarcely ever went to church. She slept either in the church porch or climbed over a hurdle (there are many hurdles instead of fences to this day in our town) into a kitchen garden. She used at least once a week to turn up "at home," that is at the house of her father's former employers, and in the winter went there every night, and slept either in the passage or the cowhouse. People were amazed that she could stand such a life, but she was accustomed to it, and, although she was so tiny, she was of a robust constitution. Some of the townspeople declared that she did all this only from pride, but that is hardly credible. She could hardly speak, and only from time to time uttered an inarticulate grunt. How could she have been proud? (Dostoyevsky, pp. 100-101.)

In her purity and her innocence, Lizaveta demonstrated a love, a trust, a sweetness that the most courageous would find desirable.

Courage is a trait that can be increased and developed. The man or woman of Christ seeks to develop this trait not for personal gain or honor but rather for the purpose of serving and blessing others.

The poet Charles Mackay said this:

> *If thou canst plan a noble deed,*
> *And never flag till it succeed,*
> *Though in the strife thy heart should bleed,*
> *Whatever obstacles control,*

Thine hour will come—go on, true soul!
Thou'lt win the prize, thou'lt reach the goal.

—Smiles, p. 445

Samuel Smiles wrote:

The courage that displays itself in silent effort and endeavor—that dares to endure all and suffer all for truth and duty—is more truly heroic than the achievements of physical valor, which are rewarded by honors and titles, or by laurels sometimes steeped in blood.

It is moral courage that characterizes the highest order of manhood and womanhood—the courage to seek and to speak the truth; the courage to be just; the courage to be honest; the courage to resist temptation; the courage to do one's duty. If men and women do not possess this virtue, they have no security whatever for the preservation of any other. (Ibid.)

He also wrote:

Women, full of tenderness and gentleness, not less than men, have in this cause been found capable of exhibiting the most unflinching courage. Such, for instance, as that of Anne Askew, who, when racked until her bones were dislocated, uttered no cry, moved no muscle, but looked her tormentors calmly in the face, and refused either to confess or to recant; or such as that of Latimer and Ridley, who, instead of bewailing their hard fate and beating their breasts, went as cheerfully to their death as a bridegroom to the altar—the one bidding the other to "be of good comfort," for that "we shall this day light such a candle in England, by God's grace, as shall never be put out;" or such, again, as that of Mary Dyer, The Quakeress, hanged by the Puritans of New England for preaching to the people, who ascended the scaffold with a willing step, and, after calmly addressing those who stood about, resigned herself into the hands of her persecutors, and died in peace and joy.

Not less courageous was the behavior of the good Sir Thomas More, who marched willingly to the scaffold, and died cheerfully there, rather than prove false to his conscience. When More had made his final decision to stand upon his principles, he felt as if he had won a victory, and said to his son-in-law Roper: "Son Roper, I thank our Lord, the field is won!" The Duke of Norfolk told him of his danger, saying: "By the mass, Master More, it is perilous striving with princes; the anger of a prince brings death!" "Is that all, my lord?" said More; "then the difference between you and me is this—that I shall die to-day, and you to-morrow." (Ibid., pp. 453-54.)

We are all aware that the time for courage will never pass. In this twentieth century we sometimes feel that we are above the ploys or cruelty of evil men. With the court system, we assume that terrible acts shall be forever eliminated. Not so. Samuel Smiles wrote in the nineteenth century:

It is a mistake to suppose that the days requiring self-sacrifice and suffering for conscience or the truth's sake are past. "Modern freedom," says Thoreau, "is only the exchange of the slavery of feudality for the slavery of opinion." The tyranny of a multitude is worse than the tyranny of an individual. How many, even in our own progressive age, have suffered persecution for bravely advocating principles and doctrines which they believed to be true? The decisions reached by counsels and conferences are but an expression of the average or popular opinion. Men of earnest thought are generally far in advance of the average sentiment. What wonder is it then that the most profound, the best, the most earnest men of every age have been men who were abused by their associates, or through charges of heresy expelled from the churches? (Ibid., pp. 456-57.)

The disciple of Christ finds the truth more sure and safe than a thousand compromises. Even though our lives be threatened, what of that? Courage and integrity stand in the breach and force the faint of heart to quail. No man of principle can let his ideals or his integrity be neutralized. The man of weakness, lacking in discipline, will everlastingly be at the mercy of every temptation. "Nothing can be more certain than that the character can only be sustained and strengthened by its own energetic action." (Ibid., p. 458.)

Everything seems to give way before those with courage. No goal will long hold off him who has persistent courage. Courage is contagious. Life without character and courage is little more than hollow existence. It brings shame, lust, and a thousand compromises. It replaces the backbone with jelly and the heart and mind with shallow hope.

Courage is steel in the backbone. It is the perpetual ally of truth. This is not to say that those of a low moral character never have courage. Some will face great danger, but their motives are selfish, and their foolish acts become an affront to the man who has a principled courage.

Aristotle said:

> The magnanimous man *will behave with moderation under both good fortune and bad.* He will know how to be exalted and how to be abased. He will neither be delighted with success nor grieved by failure. He will neither shun danger nor seek it, for there are few things which he cares for. He is reticent, and somewhat slow of speech, but speaks his mind openly and boldly when occasion calls for it. He overlooks injuries. He is not given to talk about himself or about others; for he does not care that he himself should be praised, or that other people should be blamed. He does not cry out about trifles, and craves help from none. (Ibid, p. 462; italics added.)

Courage gives magnanimity to the individual. In *Les Miserables*, Victor Hugo describes the life of Marius, the young man who eventually marries Cosette, the foster daughter of Jean Valjean. Marius is the grandson of an extremely wealthy man, but he will not accept financial help from his grandfather, as it involves what he perceives as a compromise of his integrity. Read carefully the following paragraph and ponder it. It contains pearls of exquisite thought about true courage:

> Life became stern to Marius. To eat his coats and his watch was nothing. He chewed that inexpressible thing which is called *the cud of bitterness*. A horrible thing, which includes days without bread, nights without sleep, evenings without a candle, a hearth without a fire, weeks without labour, a future without hope, a coat out at the elbows, an old hat which makes young girls laugh, the door found shut against you at night because you had not paid your rent, the insolence of the porter and the landlord, the jibes of neighbours, humiliations, self-respect outraged, any drudgery acceptable, disgust, bitterness, prostration—Marius learned how one swallows down all these things, and how they are often the only things that one has to swallow. At that period of existence, when man has need of pride, because he has need of love, he felt that he was mocked at because he was badly dressed, and ridiculed because he was poor. At the age when youth swells the heart with an imperial pride, he more than once dropped his eyes upon his wornout boots, and experienced the undeserved shame and the poignant blushes of misery. Wonderful and terrible trial, from which the feeble come out infamous, from which the strong come out sublime. Crucible into which destiny casts a man whenever she desires a soundrel or a demi-god. (Hugo, p. 573.)

Courage comes from experience, association, personal integrity, and compliance with principles based on truth, honesty, and love. Most Church members will have few opportunities to publicly show dramatic courage in the face of a great trial, but all of us have opportunity to show our braveness on personal, obscure battlefields. Every soul is engaged in hand-to-hand combat with the great deceiver, Lucifer. He has no principles, no integrity, no character, and he fights using the dirtiest of tactics. His cause is certain. He is miserable and desires that all mankind be miserable also. He is the archenemy of the soul. His greatest delight is in our destruction.

Those who have courage given them of the Lord will not fail. The proud and haughty may laugh. Those in the "great and spacious building" who mock will one day mourn. The courageous disciple of Christ will be filled with love, for love makes one courageous.

In our pursuit to become disciples of Christ, let us understand the necessity of courage. He, the Son of God, is the supreme example. His courage was love—absolute love—and His love was courage—absolute courage.

Let us live the principles suggested in this chapter to strengthen our courage. It is essential if we are to stand.

4

Wisdom

Recently I read some of the works of Robert Ingersoll, known to many as "the great agnostic." He had a beautiful way with words and seemed to have a great ability to persuade. Most of us would not want to engage someone of this man's abilities in a debate or argument. Yet, as I read his reasons for proclaiming his agnosticism, I thought, "How foolish you are." These words of Nephi rang in my mind: "O that cunning plan of the evil one! O the vainness, and the frailties, and the foolishness of men! When they are learned they think they are wise, and they hearken not unto the counsel of God, for they set it aside, supposing they know of themselves, wherefore, their wisdom is foolishness and it profiteth them not. And they shall perish. But to be learned is good if they hearken unto the counsels of God." (2 Nephi 9: 28-29.)

Robert Ingersoll undoubtedly had never been exposed to the true and living gospel of Jesus Christ. The concerns he raised about Christianity mostly referred to the apostate views and philosophies of contemporary Christian faiths. Many times as I read his arguments, I thought what a marvelous blessing the pure gospel is. In our limited inadequacies to deal with the "intellectual," we sometimes falter in defending truth. Nevertheless, I thought how elemental and shallow and limited Ingersoll

was. How foolish his brilliant mind would seem compared to the mind of any member of the Church with a
reasonable understanding of the gospel! Every argument
he propounded could be answered with gospel knowledge. I wondered how much exposure he had had to the
restored gospel of Jesus Christ. He could have found so
many answers to his quest for truth.

Elder John H. Vandenberg said, "The fruit of wisdom
ripens slowly." Learning is good when we hearken unto
the counsels of God. What a profound influence every
teacher, every leader, every parent has on young and old
alike. We sometimes feel that when our stone is tossed
into the pond it simply sinks to the bottom without caus-
ing a continuous rippling effect. We feel that our realm of
influence is so limited that it simply does not make any
difference to anyone.

Let me bear my testimony that indeed every life does
make a difference for good or for evil. In the sixteenth
century, one of the wisest men who ever lived, Desiderius
Erasmus, stated, "To be a schoolmaster is next to being a
king. Do you count it lowly employment to imbue the
minds of young people with the love of Christ and the
best of literature, and to return them to their country honest and virtuous men? In the opinion of fools it is a humble task, but in fact it is the noblest of occupations." He
spoke truly.

What of Ingersoll, then? This man with great reser-
voirs of knowledge and superior intellect will someday
come to a full knowledge of the consequences of his er-
rors. Great knowledge he did have, but wisdom he had
little. There will one day come to him, on the other side of
the veil, those who will accuse him as the one who led
them away from the simple faith they had learned, a faith
generated by common, simple folks with not much

knowledge but with sufficient wisdom to believe, through faith, and to follow the simple Carpenter of Galilee.

Wouldn't it be marvelous if we could live so as to be the truly good example. Dr. D. Bruck Lockerbie, dean of the faculty of the Stony Brook School, spoke to a group of teachers at Mastic Beach, New York. He concluded his inspiring discourse with this:

> I've watched with fascination this winter Bill Moyer's series on P.B.S. called "Creativity." Perhaps you remember the first program with Maya Angelou and her return to her childhood home of Stamps, Arkansas. That program ended with Miss Angelou speaking to a classroom of children in that tiny and culturally abandoned village. Her final words to them—this cosmopolitan woman, this artist, this poet, this person who must have seemed to those children like a creature from another planet—her benediction upon them was this: "When I look at you, I see who I was. When you look at me, I hope you see who you can become." (*Vital Speeches*, May 15, 1982.)

Where is wisdom? The man or woman of Christ places an inestimable value on obtaining knowledge and intelligence (which is the ability to use knowledge with wisdom).

We must work to obtain knowledge and wisdom. We cannot teach and train what we have neither learned nor experienced. Consider this example of Robert Nicoll as an exercise in learning wisdom:

> Robert Nicoll wrote to a friend, after reading the "Recollections of Coleridge," "What a mighty intellect was lost in that man for want of a little energy—a little determination!" Nicoll himself was a true and brave spirit, who died young, but not before he had encountered and overcome great difficulties in life. At his outset, while carrying on a small business as a bookseller, he found himself weighed down with a debt of only twenty pounds, which he said he felt "weighing like a millstone round his neck," and that "if he had it paid he never would borrow again from mor-

tal man." Writing to his mother at the time he said, "Fear not for me, dear mother, for I feel myself daily growing firmer and more hopeful in spirit. The more I think and reflect—and thinking, not reading, is now my occupation—I feel that, whether I be growing richer or not, I am growing a wiser man, which is far better. Pain, poverty, and all the other wild beasts in life which so frighten others, I am so bold as to think I could look in the face without shrinking, without losing respect for myself, faith in man's high destinies, or trust in God. There is a point which it costs much mental toil and struggling to gain, but which, when once gained, a man can look down from, as a traveler from a lofty mountain, on storms raging below, while he is walking in sunshine. That I have yet gained this point in life I will not say, but I feel myself daily nearer to it." (Smiles, pp. 308-9.)

Samuel Smiles wrote the following:

We learn wisdom from failure much more than from success. We often discover what *will* do by finding out what will not do; and probably he who never made a mistake never made a discovery. (Ibid., p. 310.)
The very greatest things—great thoughts, great discoveries, inventions—have usually been nurtured in hardship, often pondered over in sorrow, and at length established with difficulty. (Ibid., p. 310.)
"Sweet indeed are the uses of adversity." They reveal to us our powers, and call forth our energies. If there be real worth in the character, like sweet herbs, it will give forth its finest fragrance when pressed. (Ibid., p. 311.)

Wisdom, however, would dictate that the teacher of youth not emasculate the simple truths and faith, learned at home from experience, by using "superior" intellect and knowledge to throw mental obstacles into their path before they have the mental maturity to reason, ponder, and grow. It is not superior intellect but cowardice to mentally or spiritually maim or cripple those who are still innocent and vulnerable and who do not have the mature mental capacity to fight the giants of deceit. This may be one of the reasons the Lord does not allow Satan to tempt children until they come to the age of accountability. Thank God for men and women of wisdom who create healthy climates of mental growth toward wisdom. An atmosphere of protecting the true, eternal principles with faith is vital until the root has sufficient strength.

Og Mandino's bestseller *The Greatest Salesman in the World* contains some choice statements. One of the great principles of success written in his book is on his first "scroll." Apply this principle to your quest for wisdom: "Today I will pluck grapes of wisdom from the tallest and fullest vines in the vineyard, for these were planted by the wisest ... who have come before me, generation upon generation." (Mandino, pp. 57-58.)

Coleridge says that wisdom is "common sense in an uncommon degree." Spurgeon states that it is "the right use of knowledge," and Francis Hutcheson defines it as "the pursuing of the best ends by the best means."

President Stephen L Richards wrote, "I define wisdom as being the beneficent application of knowledge in decision. I think of wisdom not in the abstract but as functional. Life is largely made up of choices and determinations. That at least is true of intelligent living, and I can think of no wisdom that does not contemplate the good of man and society." (Richards, p. 67.) I wonder what Ingersoll would think of the above statements. Would he suppose that leading men and women away from a faith in Christ is a "beneficent application" of knowledge?

We learn wisdom in our communications with each other. Samuel Smiles wrote much about this kind of wisdom:

> It is necessary to one's personal happiness, to exercise control over one's words as well as acts: for there are words that strike even harder than blows; and men may

"speak daggers," though they use none. The stinging re-
partee that rises to the lips, and which, if uttered, might
cover an adversary with confusion, how difficult it sometimes is to resist saying it! "Heaven keeps us," says Miss
Bremer, in her "Home," "from the destroying power of
words!" There are words which sever hearts more than
sharp swords do; there are words the point of which sting
the heart through the course of a whole life.

Thus character exhibits itself in self-control of speech
as much as in anything else. The wise and forbearant man
will restrain his desire to say a smart or severe thing at the
expense of another's feelings; while the fool blurts out
what he thinks, and will sacrifice his friend rather than his
joke. Even statesmen might be named, who have failed
through their inability to resist the temptation of saying
clever and spiteful things at their adversary's expense.
"The turn of a sentence," says Bentham, "has decided the
fate of many a friendship, and, for aught that we know, the
fate of many a kingdom." So, when one is tempted to
write a clever but harsh thing, though it may be difficult to
restrain it, it is always better to leave it in the inkstand. "A
goose's quill," says the Spanish proverb, "often hurts
more than a lion's claw."

Carlyle says, when speaking of Oliver Cromwell, "He
that can not withal keep his mind to himself, can not practice any considerable thing whatsoever." It was said of
William the Silent, by one of his greatest enemies, that an
arrogant or indiscreet word was never known to fall from
his lips. Like him, Washington was discretion itself in the
use of speech, never taking advantage of an opponent or
seeking a short-lived triumph in a debate. And it is said
that, in the long run, the world comes round to and sup-
ports the wise man who knows when and how to be silent.

We have heard men of great experience say that they
have often regretted having spoken, but never once regretted holding their tongue. "Be silent," says Pythagoras,
"or say something better than silence." "Speak fitly," says
George Herbert, "or be silent wisely." St. Francis de Sales,
whom Leigh Hunt styled "the Gentleman Saint," has said:
"It is better to remain silent than to speak the truth ill-
humoredly, and so spoil an excellent dish by covering it
with bad sauce." Another Frenchman, Lacordaire, charac-

teristically puts speech first, and silence next. "After speech," he said, "silence is the greatest power in the world." Yet a word spoken in season, how powerful it may be! As the old Welch proverb has it, "A golden tongue is in the mouth of the blessed." . . .

Remember, "The best corrective of intolerance in disposition is increase of wisdom and enlarged experiences of life. Cultivated good sense will usually save men from the entanglements in which moral impatience is apt to involve them; good sense consisting chiefly in that temper of mind which enables its possessor to deal with the practical affairs of life with justice, judgment, discretion, and charity. Hence men of culture and experience are invariably found the most forebearant and tolerant, as ignorant and narrow-minded persons are found the most unforgiving and intolerant. Men of large and generous natures, in proportion to their practical wisdom, are disposed to make allowance for the defects and disadvantages of others—allowance for the controlling power of circumstances in the formation of character, and the limited power of resistance of weak and fallible natures to temptation and error. "I see no fault committed," said Goethe, "which I also might not have committed." (Smiles, pp. 482-85.)

Wisdom is a worthy goal for all. No truly great leader can long survive without a goodly portion of it. Wisdom demands courage. The wise thing is not always the popular thing. The thoughts and actions of a wise man or woman would be foreign to the normal thoughts that pervade our minds. The wise person must be able to see things in their true perspective. He must be able to understand the long-range implications and consequences of our statements and actions. The Hebrew prayer book, Ethics of the Fathers, tells us: "There are seven marks of an uncultured and seven of a wise man. The wise man does not speak before him who is greater than he in wisdom; and does not break in upon the speech of his fellow; he is not hasty to answer; he speaks upon the first thing first and upon the last last; regarding that which he has not understood he says, 'I do not understand it' and he acknowledges the truth. The reverse of all this is to be found in an uncultured man." (*Vital Speeches,* Jan. 15, 1981, p. 529.)

Ronald W. Raskin, president of the University of Nebraska, stated, "Who is wise? All of us, if we continue to care about learning and to learn about caring, for that is the essence of wisdom." (Ibid.)

Many years ago as a struggling young executive I determined to put on my office wall a quotation that would be a constant reminder to me, as well as to all who entered my office, of what is really important in life. After weeks of thought I finally decided upon a passage in the book of Micah, chapter 6, verse 8: "He hath shewed thee, O man, what is good; and what doth the Lord require of thee, but to do justly, and to love mercy, and to walk humbly with thy God." Oh, the wisdom in such a few words.

In the early days of the Church, a handful of faithful men and women of wisdom and integrity were persecuted on all sides. They were wise enough to know that the work of God would succeed, that no power on earth or in hell could frustrate God's holy plans. They held steadfast and were true. Now that splendid band of a few has expanded to millions upon millions who are possessors of the wisdom of God revealed through his holy prophets. Let us seek for a wise and understanding heart, for truly this is essential to the disciple of Christ.

5

Christian Service

When we returned from presiding over the Texas San Antonio Mission, I went through a complete physical, including a test for tuberculosis. The test proved positive.

It was interesting what took place in my mind. I love my wife, children, grandchildren, and other family members more than my own life. If I had tuberculosis, every contact I made with my family could jeopardize them. How could I hug my children, hold them close, and kiss them? How could I hold my daughter in my arms? How could I have physical contact with my son? How could I embrace and kiss my wife?

I decided to tell my wife and then simply suffer in silence. I decided to let the Brethren know so they could release me rather than risk impairing the health of one soul. Now, I realize these were emotional thoughts, and one can be healed from tuberculosis. But these issues were real and of great concern to me. A doctor with a sophisticated knowledge of the disease might not have considered my worries as legitimate concerns. Nonetheless, I was greatly troubled.

I phoned the doctor and told him of the positive results of the test. I went to his office, underwent a series of X rays, and took other tests. I did not have tuberculosis; I had only been exposed to it. A great burden was taken from my heart. But for a few short days I was making decisions that might affect me for the rest of my life. Unquestionably they would have forced a change in conduct and could have affected much of what I was doing.

I will never forget those days. The doctors suggested that my exposure came from contact with some of our beloved Mexican-American brethren along the Texas-Mexico border, where conditions are sometimes so deplorable that tuberculosis and other respiratory diseases occur. If I had known before what I knew after, would I have withheld my hugs and embraces for these brethren? No, even if I had contracted tuberculosis I would not have treated them differently. I love them. How could I withhold that love and warmth over concern for self? I do not think that is what Jesus would have me do.

I shook hands with members of the Church at the leper colony in Kalaupapa, Hawaii. At the time I did not know that the disease was arrested. It didn't make any difference. I did what I thought Jesus would have me do. I shook hands with each one in love and compassion. We should be engaged in true Christian service.

Mother Teresa, a Catholic nun who received the Nobel Peace Prize in December 1979, said this in her clumsy but eloquent English:

> We read . . . in the Gospel very clearly—love as I have loved you—as I love you—as the Father has loved me, I love you—and the harder the Father loved him, he gave him to us, and how much we love one another, we, too, must give each other until it hurts. It is not enough for us to say: I love God, but I do not love my neighbour. . . .
>
> We have been created to love and be loved, and then [Jesus] has become a man to make it possible for us to love as he loved us. He makes himself the hungry one—the naked one—the homeless one—the sick one—the one in prision—the lonely one— the unwanted one— and he says: You did it to me. Hungry for our love, and

this is the hunger of our poor people. This is the hunger that you and I must find, it may be in our own home. . . .

The poor are very wonderful people. One evening we went out and we picked up four people from the street. And one of them was in a most terrible condition—and I told the sisters: You take care of the other three, I take care of this one that looked worse. So I did for her all that my love can do. I put her in bed, and there was such a beautiful smile on her face. She took hold of my hand, as she said one word only: Thank you—and she died.

I could not help but examine my conscience before her, and I asked what would I say if I was in her place. And my answer was very simple. I would have tried to draw a little attention to myself, I would have said I am hungry, that I am dying, I am cold, I am in pain, or something, but she gave me much more—she gave me her grateful love. And she died with a smile on her face.

As that man whom we picked up from the drain, half eaten with worms, and we brought him to the home. "I have lived like an animal in the street, but I am going to die like an angel, loved and cared for." And it was so wonderful to see the greatness of that man who could speak like that, who could die like that without blaming anybody, without cursing anybody, without comparing anything. Like an angel—that is the greatness of our people. And that is why we believe what Jesus has said: I was hungry—I was naked—I was homeless—I was unwanted, unloved, uncared for—and you did it to me. . . .

I had the most extraordinary experience with a Hindu family who had eight children. A gentleman came to our house and said: Mother Teresa, there is a family with eight children, they had not eaten for so long—do something. So I took some rice and I went there immediately. And I saw the children—their eyes shining with hunger—I don't know if you have ever seen hunger. But I have seen it very often. And she took the rice, she divided the rice, and she went out. When she came back I asked her—where did you go, what did you do? And she gave me a very simple answer: "They are hungry also." What struck me most was that she knew—and who are they, a Muslim family—and she knew.

I didn't bring more rice that evening because I wanted them to enjoy the joy of sharing. But there was those children, radiating joy, sharing the joy with their mother because she had the love to give. As you see this is where love begins—at home. (*Vital Speeches,* June 1, 1980.)

The disciple of Christ is a person of total love and empathy. Discipleship is not easy. It brings weariness, exhaustion, and fatigue. Often it requires that we travel alone. The call of discipleship may take us to slums and poverty, to the sick and dying, to the heavy-hearted and desperate. It may take us through deep waters, or refining fires, but always we have the promise of peace, joy, assurance, trust, and success that come to those who walk in His footsteps.

Recently I flew home from a mission presidents' seminar. I had been up about seventeen hours. I changed into my sleep wear and climbed into bed beside my wife. We talked for a few moments, and then the phone rang.

A boyhood friend, one I had known since first grade, was on the line. "Brother Vaughn," he said in a trembling voice, "my daughter is back in the hospital. She has had several major seizures. She has stopped breathing twice. She is on oxygen but seems to be failing fast." I asked if she had been administered to. He said, "No, we were hoping you could come and bless her."

The physical body was tired. I felt I had earned the rest. I also felt that my wife needed me, and the flesh wavered. However, the spirit knew precisely what was to be done. I said, "Joe, I will be there in about thirty minutes." (We live about half an hour away from the University of Utah Medical Center.) I turned to my wife, Merlene, and asked her if she would like to go. This noble woman said yes. We both got up, got dressed, and drove to the hospital.

I embraced this sweet friend that I had known for over forty-six years. We found a little room and along with family members joined in a prayer of great faith.

Then Joe and I went into the intensive-care room and gave his daughter a blessing. We pleaded with the Lord and had a sweet, peaceful assurance come over us that she was in His care. At the time we gave the blessing, I wondered whether or not she would even live through it.

Merlene had waited in the car. We drove home and were not tired or exhausted any more. We were deeply grateful to have been called upon.

Opportunities for Christian acts of service do not always come at convenient times. Approximately two or three years ago I was in Southern California. I had reorganized a stake. As I was getting ready to go out to the airport where I could relax and just let down, a woman approached me. She said, "Elder Featherstone, are you going back to Salt Lake today?" I said yes. She continued, "Are you going on that four o'clock Western Airlines flight?" I responded that I was. Then she said, "Would you mind doing a favor for me?" I quickly thought about the schedule I had just been through; my body was begging for a little break. I assumed she wanted me to hand-carry something to a relative. I never check baggage unless I absolutely have to. I wondered if I would have to check what it was I assumed she wanted me to bring back. I thought about waiting at the baggage claim for the item, and then I wondered where it would need to be delivered. Then the Spirit thrust aside all empty excuses, and I responded as a service-oriented leader should.

I said, "I will be glad to help in whatever way possible." Then the woman said, "My grandson Phillip has been down here with me for a couple of weeks. How would you like to baby-sit him home to Salt Lake? His mother will be waiting for him at the airport." We arranged to meet at the Los Angeles Airport, where the grandmother introduced me to Phillip. Just before we boarded the plane, she said, "Here is an envelope. Will you wait until you are on the plane to open it?"

Phillip and I boarded the plane. We sat on the front row behind the bulkhead. A man was in the window seat, Phillip was in the middle seat, and I was seated on the aisle. We fastened our seat belts, and the man sitting next to Phillip said, "Hello, little boy." Phillip turned to me and said, "I don't like him." I turned to the man and said, "He's not my son."

The Lord seems to give children a special purity that lets them know when people are genuine. I looked more carefully at the man and thought Phillip was probably right.

I reached into my pocket and opened the letter from the grandmother. It went something like this.

> Dear Elder Featherstone,
> Thank you for taking Phillip back to Salt Lake City and baby-sitting him for us. We appreciate it. His mother will be there at the airport to meet you; but if she is not there, then here is what you do.

And she gave some instructions. Then she wrote:

> The reason I did not dare have you open the letter before you were on board the plane is that I did not have enough courage to ask you to do another favor for us. Phillip's brother Ricky is in the University of Utah hospital. He has had constant seizures, many a day. The doctors do not know what else to do. They have done all they know and he still has the problem. Do you think you could possibly find time to go by the hospital and give him a blessing?

When we arrived in Salt Lake City we disembarked from our flight. No one met us at the gate. We walked the length of the terminal, and still no one recognized Phillip. We went down the escalator, past the baggage claim, and out to the curbside. I have done some unusual things in my life, but I wondered what Merlene would say when I came home from a stake conference visit and brought a small boy with me.

I looked around and stood with Phillip for a moment, and then the mother pulled up along the curb. They had been delayed in coming to the airport. The sweet mother was very kind, and she loaded a happy Phillip and all his gear into the car.

A little later I was standing in one of the pediatric wards at the University of Utah hospital. There were about six little children in cribs. An attendant was mopping the floor, and then he left the room. I was all alone in the hospital room with these beautiful children.

I found out which one was Ricky and went over to him. I said, "My name is Vaughn Featherstone. Do you know who I just left?" He said, "No," and I said, "I came back from Los Angeles today and brought your brother Phillip home. I told him I was coming up here to see you." Ricky was only about four, but tears came to his eyes. He missed his little brother.

Then I said to him, "Ricky, I am a friend of President Spencer W. Kimball, and he loves you. President Kimball is a prophet and I am his friend. Your grandmother asked me if I would give you a blessing. Do you know what it means when someone lays his hands on your head and gives you a blessing?" He said, "Yes." And then I said, "Ricky, do you believe in Jesus?" He said, "Yes." "Do you know that Jesus loves you? Do you know that Jesus can heal you?" He answered, "Yes." Then I asked, "Would you like me to give you a blessing and heal you?" "Yes," he said.

I laid my hands upon his head and gave Ricky a blessing. An interesting thing happened in the little pediatric ward. The other children stopped playing and crying and seemed to listen.

When I finished the blessing I reached into my pocket and pulled out a beautifully polished rock with my name on it that someone had given me. I gave it to Ricky so that when his mother came she would know I had been there.

Two years later I was in the Kingsport Tennessee Stake. A sweet young mother came up to me after conference. She told me it was her mother that had asked me to baby-sit Phillip and bless Ricky. Then she said, "Have you ever had any feedback on your blessing?" I told her I had not. Then she shared with me the great miracle: "Ricky did not have another seizure after you gave him the blessing, nor has he had one since."

It was not opportune to take Phillip home, nor was it convenient to drop by the University of Utah Medical Center; but it was what Jesus would have done. Our service must always lead us to ask, "What would Jesus do?"

Recently I was called by a close friend who told me his father had passed away. I expressed my sympathy and asked when the funeral would be. When he told me, I looked at my calendar and said, "I would love to be at the funeral to honor your great father and to express my love and sympathy to your mom. But I am getting ready to leave town and I am swamped that day." He said, "Well, we talked about that and figured that your schedule would be too busy to ask you to speak, but Dad had suggested that if you were available you might do it." It is interesting how suddenly everything on my calendar could be adjusted. I said, "You tell your mom I will be there." After the funeral I received this letter: "The last few months, Dad knew his time was short here on this earth. One day when we were talking about funeral arrangements, I asked him who he would like to have speak at his service. He said, 'I surely would like to have Brother Featherstone, but I know that as busy as he is that isn't possible.' Then he went on to mention some other good men. When I learned of your coming to speak, I shed many tears of joy. I just couldn't believe with all your many duties and responsibilities that you would come."

Then I realized what this service on my part meant to her. She closed by saying, "I wonder how the Lord can be so good to me."

Now you and I both understand it was not having Vaughn Featherstone speak but rather having a dying husband's wish granted that filled her with this great love for the Lord.

Think of all the opportunities you will have to serve at inconvenient times. I promise that most of the service you render to the Lord will come at times not convenient to you.

Edward Markham wrote a poem entitled "How the Great Guest Came." It demonstrates beautifully what I am trying to say.

> Before the cathedral in grandeur rose
> At Ingelburg where the Danube goes;
> Before its forest of silver spires
> Went airily up to the clouds and fires;
> Before the oak had ready a beam,
> While yet the arch was stone and dream—
> There where the altar was later laid,
> Conrad, the cobbler, plied his trade.
>
> It happened one day at the year's white end—
> Two neighbors called on their old-time friend;
> And they found the shop, so meager and mean,
> Made gay with a hundred boughs of green.
> Conrad was stitching with face ashine,
> But suddenly stopped as he twitched a twine;
> "Old friends, good news! At dawn today,

His friends went home; and his face grew still
As he watched for the shadow across the sill.
He lived all the moments o'er and o'er,
When the Lord should enter the lowly door—
The knock, the call, the latch pulled up,
The lighted face, the offered cup.
He would wash the feet where the spikes had been,
He would kiss the hands where the nails went in,
And then at the last would sit with Him
And break the bread as they day grew dim.

While the cobbler mused there passed his pane
A beggar drenched by the driving rain.
He called him in from the stony street
And gave him shoes for his bruised feet.
The beggar went and there came a crone,
Her face with wrinkles of sorrow sown,
A bundle of fagots bowed her back,
And she was spent with the wrench and rack.
He gave her his loaf and steadied her load
As she took her way on the weary road.
Then to his door came a little child,
Lost and afraid in the world so wild,
In the big, dark world. Catching it up,
He gave it milk in the waiting cup,
And led it home to its mother's arms,
Out of the reach of the world's alarms.

The day went down in the crimson west
And with it the hope of the blessed Guest,
And Conrad sighed as the world turned gray:
"Why is it, Lord, that your feet delay?
Did You forget that this was the day?"
Then soft in the silence a Voice he heard:

"Lift up your heart, for I kept my word.
Three times I came to your friendly door;
Three times my shadow was on your floor.
I was the beggar with bruised feet;
I was the woman you gave to eat;
I was the child on the homeless street!"

—Felleman, pp. 296-97

We must determine to serve one another. We must listen to the spirit when the flesh is weak. The Master said truly, "Inasmuch as ye have done it unto one of the least of these my brethren, ye have done it unto me." (Matthew 25:40.) The blessings are tenfold for the acts of Christian service we do even when it is not convenient.

6
Respect for the Individual

Each one of us is different. A myriad of different influences fashion and mold us. We do not think alike or at the same speed. A husband and wife may live together for half a century and still not fully understand each other.

Years ago I read a book by a felon in a state penitentiary. When he was only a boy, his mother and father had decided to divorce. One night they were arguing about who would take what after the divorce. The boy was in a neighboring room and overheard the conversation. He could not see their facial expressions; he knew only what he heard.

As I recall, there was a long silence and then the father said, "You take the boy." The boy loved his father, and this just about destroyed him. He felt that his father simply did not want him or the responsibility. Apparently the mother, who was more of a social gadabout than most mothers, sighed and resigned herself to her fate. The boy grew up with his mother, never letting her know that he had overheard the discussion.

Years later, after his imprisonment, he confronted his father with the story. I do not remember the exact conversation from the book, but it went something like this: "Dad, I always thought you loved me more than Mother did when I was growing up. And yet, when it came time to decide with whom I would live, you didn't want me. You had her take me. I never felt that she really wanted me either. When I found out you didn't care, my whole world crashed in on me."

The father told the son something that would have changed his whole life if he had only known. He told him that when it came time to decide who would take the boy, he thought his heart would break. The most precious thing in his life was his son. He thought about the boy and decided he would be happier with his mother. He thought this was the greatest personal sacrifice he could make for his son. He put all of his emotions, feelings, and love on the altar. But the great, open cavity of suffering could not be healed.

So often we go through great personal sacrifices for our families but are misunderstood. Most men carry their emotions deep inside. I once met a man, not a member of the Church, who told me his wife had suggested divorce. Eventually they were divorced, but during the "talking" times she told him she wanted him at home more. His job was too demanding, and she would rather have had him work a forty-hour week and spend more time at home. He replied, "I would never work this hard for myself. I am working this hard so you and the children will be proud of me. I put in long hours to increase my pay so we can have the nice things you have always wanted." He thought she understood. She thought he was doing it for himself. So his pure motive, in error or not, was hidden all those months. He did eventually stop working such long hours, but not soon enough, and they were divorced. What a tragedy that a man and a woman could not really communicate and know each other's hearts.

It has been my counsel to couples over the years to always ask questions. Lay aside the accusations until you are satisfied that the necessary questions have been asked. This is wisdom. In our relationships with our family members, we should remember always to be Christian. What would happen if every woman would treat her husband the way she would the Prophet if he were in their home? What would happen if every man would be as considerate, thoughtful, and kind to his wife as he would the Prophet's wife if she were in their home?

A man and woman are greatly influenced by each other in their marriage. The influence can be for good and create a blossoming love with the sweetest fragrance and peace, or it can be a most damning experience that generates heartache and sickness of soul. And a couple's relationship always has a profound effect on their children.

A member of a stake presidency recently told this story at a stake conference: A sweet family had a young neighbor boy who spent a great deal of time in their home. Let us refer to him as Jeff. Quite often he would need to be reminded to go home when it was getting late. One particular night at a late hour the good father suggested that Jeff ought to be on his way home. Jeff asked him if he could stay a little longer so that he would not have to go home before his father arrived. "Isn't your mother home?" "Yes, but I would sure like to stay until my father comes home." "Why don't you call home and see if your father is there yet?" "I know he isn't; he is down at a bar. Could I use your phone to call him there?"

The boy knew the number without even looking it up. He dialed the number and eventually got his father on the phone. The one-sided conversation went like this: "Daddy, how soon are you coming home? Can I stay here until you come home? Please, Daddy. No, she's drunk and I don't want to go home until you get there. Do I have to,

Daddy? Please let me stay. Will you come right home? Please hurry, Daddy." And with this Jeff hung up the phone.

Then he said, "Daddy says I have to go home. Thanks for letting me stay for a while." With a lonely, crushed look in his eyes, Jeff walked out into the night and went home.

Jeff's family moved from the neighborhood, and the family said, "We wonder what Jeff is doing now. Was there a divorce? Will Jeff be able to retain his innocent purity, or is he so surrounded by alcohol and all its vices that the satanic quicksand will pull him under? What chance will he have as a teenager?"

Contrast this with a father who had to discipline his young son. He paddled the boy and sent him to his room. A little later, wanting to "show forth an increase of love" toward him whom he had reproved, he went upstairs to his son's room. He stood in the doorway and looked in. His young son, with tear-stained cheeks, was sitting in the window seat. He had his trucks and stuffed animals gathered around him. He was deeply sad and all alone. He looked up and saw his father standing in the doorway. The son picked up a large truck in one arm and a stuffed animal in the other and said, "These are the things I love most." The father walked across the room, took the truck out of one arm, the stuffed animal out of the other arm, and picked up his boy and hugged him tight. Then the son said, "But Daddy, I love you most of all."

We must always respect the individual. Samuel Smiles wrote, "The cultivation of all parts of the moral and intellectual nature is requisite to form the man or woman of healthy and well-balanced character. Without sympathy or consideration for others, man were a poor, stunted, sordid, selfish being; and without cultivated intelligence, the most beautiful woman were little better than a well-dressed doll." (Smiles, p. 558.)

Communication is essential in our relationships, if we truly love. Love is not jealousy, control, dominion, or power. Love is a reflection of attitudes toward a person that tempers and subdues unworthy thoughts and actions. Among the synonyms for *love* are the following: tender feeling, regard, demonstrativeness, sentimentality, natural affection, adoration, and hundreds more.

I like what David Starr Jordan says about love: "Love, too, is a positive word. Not love,—but loving. And loving brings happiness only as it works itself out into living action. The love that would end in no helping act and no purpose or responsibility is a mere torture of the mind." (Jordan, p. 13.)

I appreciate his insight that love, *true* love, demands action. It requires positive, virtuous, serving action.

Every positive, loving act is a communication that blesses all involved. It fills the soul of the recipient and replenishes the soul of the giver. The felon approaching his father did not understand his father's love. He could not have seen or known of the personal sacrifice the father felt as he suggested that the boy go with his mother.

Noncommunication is destructive. It leads to misjudgments, poor calculations, misunderstanding, and contention. Oh, the relief that would come to families who have not communicated if only they could, through love, learn to truly know and understand each other's feelings.

Much heartsickness and evil could be avoided if we would take time to communicate. David Starr Jordan states, "Temptation resisted strengthens the mind and the soul. Not to escape temptation, but to master it, is the way of righteousness." (Ibid., p. 14.)

The same is true about communication: we should not

attempt to escape from it but to master it. David Starr Jordan goes on to say, "Innocence is not necessarily virtue, and may be farther from it than vice itself. We may call no man virtuous till he has passed from innocence to the conquest of tempatation. Any fool may be innocent. It takes a wise man to be virtuous." (Ibid., pp. 14-15.)

Mr. Jordan relates a powerful example of lack of communication:

> In a recent journal, Mr. William C. Morrow tells a story of a clergyman and a vagabond. They met by chance on the street, where the very incongruity of their lives drew them together. Each was tempted by the other. The young student of divinity, fresh from the seminary, in black broadcloth and unspotted necktie, seemed to the vagabond so pure, so clean, so innocent, that suddenly his soul arose in revolt against his past life, his vulgar surroundings, his squalid future. The inspiration of the unspoiled example gave him strength to resist. For a moment, at least, he threw off the chains which years of weakness had fastened upon him. The clergyman, on the other hand, found a fascination in sin. It seemed to come to him as an illumination of the realities of life, a contrast to a life of empty words and dry asceticism. All the yearning curiosity of his suppressed impulses called out for the freedom of the vagabond. His mouth watered for the untasted fruits of life. These unkown joys seemed to him the only joys there were. He had never known temptation, and hence had never resisted it. To his innocence, the cheap meanness of sin was not revealed.
>
> As it chanced, so the story goes, when next the pair met, the vagabond and the minister, they had exchanged places. From the curbstone pulpit, the vagabond spoke to his fellow sinners in words that burned, for they came from the fulness of his experience. He had met the Devil face to face, and could speak as one who knew him, and who would, if he could, cast off his horrid chains. As he went on with his harangue, the other came up, dishevelled of garment and unsteady of step, his speech reeking with foulness and profanity. The pleasures of sin were his for the season, and the policeman led him on to the city

jail to sober up. There he would have leisure to cast up the account in the bitterness which follows unresisted temptation. (Ibid., pp. 15-16.)

What a different story this might have been if the young minister had carefully interviewed the vagabond who knew that endlessly and forever wickedness never was happiness. Those who do not communicate must pay the price.

To respect the dignity of the individual requires communication and self-respect. It requires a sense of self-worth, which comes from keeping commitments, serving others, exercising faith in Christ, and living a virtuous life of integrity. Dignity adds majesty to the character.

Let me conclude with some personal feelings. We all love our bishops, stake presidents, and the General Authorities and other Church leaders. It is my feeling that as one leader is released and another called, our allegiance follows the mantle. We all love the Prophet of this great church, but when he passes away, our love and allegiance will transfer to the next man the Lord would have lead this kingdom. This does not diminish the individual but rather gives us insight into the Lord's order of calling his leaders. In other words, not one of us should have one particle of false pride in any calling we receive in the Church. And when we are honored by Church members, we must remember that we are being honored because we temporarily wear the mantle of a particular call. Should that call be extended to someone else, then that person would receive the honor. But this does not take away from the dignity of the individual who has kept the commandments and lived gospel principles. That dignity and self-worth can never be removed.

We are our Father in heaven's spirit children, and we can become like Him. Every soul that has lived, does live,

or will live had or has that potential. That is the dignity of
the individual. We can become like our Father in heaven,
and we do control our own destiny in these things.

7

Righteous Influence

A noted psychologist, Dr. Alan Loy McGinnis, shared the following case history: "A new patient was sitting in my chair and I asked about his child-hood. 'Was it happy?' 'No, not really,' he said. 'My dad was a man's man, and worked in a factory. He never had much to say. He was interested in sports and I wasn't well-coordinated and didn't go out for sports, and I just never felt I could please him. Then, several years after he had died, I went home to visit my mom and I was talking to some of his old cronies from the plant, and they told me how he used to brag about me at work. I was flab-bergasted. I had no idea he felt that way about me.'" (McGinnis, p. 376.)

What a sad story. Now read this quotation, "About School," and compare the tragic consequences of both.

> He always wanted to say things. But no one understood.
> He always wanted to explain things. But no one cared.
> So he drew.
> Sometimes he would just draw and it wasn't anything. He wanted to carve it in stone or write it in the sky.
> He would lie out on the grass and look up in the sky and it would be only him and the sky and things inside him that needed saying.
> And it was after that, that he drew the picture. It was a beautiful picture.
> He kept it under the pillow and would let no one see it.

And he would look at it every night and think about it. And when it was dark, and his eyes were closed, he could still see it.

And it was all of him. And he loved it.

When he started school he brought it with him. Not to show anyone, but just to have with him like a friend.

It was funny about school.

He sat in a square, brown desk like all the other square, brown desks, and he thought it should be red.

And his room was a square, brown room. Like all the other rooms. And it was tight and close. And stiff.

He hated to hold the pencil and the chalk, with his arm stiff and his feet flat on the floor, stiff, with the teacher watching and watching.

And then he had to write numbers. And they weren't anything. They were worse than the letters that could be something if you put them together.

And the numbers were tight and square and he hated the whole thing.

The teacher came and spoke to him. She told him to wear a tie like all the other boys. He said he didn't like them and she said it didn't matter.

After that they drew. And he drew all yellow and it was the way he felt about the morning. And it was beautiful.

The teacher came and smiled at him. "What's this?" she said. "Why don't you draw something like Ken's drawing? Isn't that beautiful?"

It was all questions.

After that his mother bought him a tie and he always drew airplanes and rocket ships like everyone else. And he threw the old picture away.

And when he lay out alone looking at the sky, it was big and all of everything, but he wasn't any more.

He was square inside and brown, and his hands were stiff, and he was like everyone else. And the thing inside him that needed saying didn't need saying any more.

It had stopped pushing. It was crushed. Stiff.

Like everything else. (*Vital Speeches,* Sept. 15, 1982, pp. 278-79.)

Oh, the pity of a world that seems obsessed with the desire to neutralize everyone.

Influence is a part of every life. Some exercise it, and

we all respond to it. What a divine blessing are those who
have it and use it for good. Influence is a force that all
people recognize. Parents and teachers have a power
through influence that can alter, modify, or direct children and youth toward success or failure.

I remember a story told by President David O. McKay
regarding a boy whose bedroom was in the basement.
The boy had such bad feelings toward his cruel father that
each evening when the father returned from work and
walked across the floor, the boy would jump up and run
to the toilet and regurgitate. The father could never find it
in his heart a good or loving word. Always he criticized.
Thank God for being the Father of our spirits. We do have
a resiliency that is part of us. Even the weakest soul does
not break without great pressure over a long period of
time.

Years ago I was sitting in Marv Abrams's office. Marv
was a business associate of mine. On his wall was a
framed copy of a last will and testament found in the
pocket of an old, ragged coat belonging to one of the insane patients of a Chicago poorhouse. According to Bar-
bara Boyd in the *Washington Law Reporter,* the man had
been a lawyer and the will was written in a firm hand on
a few scraps of paper. So unusual was it that it was sent to
another attorney; and so impressed was he with its con-
tents that he read it before the Chicago Bar Association,
and a resolution was passed ordering it probated. It is
now in the records of Cook County, Illinois:

> I, Charles Lounsberry, being of sound and disposing
> mind and memory, do hereby make and publish this my
> last will and testament, in order, as justly may be, to distri-
> bute any interest in the world among succeeding men.
> That part of my interests which is known in law and
> recognized in the sheepbound volumes as my property,
> being inconsiderable and of none account, I make no dis-

position of in this, my will. My right to live, being but a life estate, is not at my disposal, but, these things excepted all else in the world I now proceed to devise and bequeath.

Item: I give to good fathers and mothers, in trust, for their children, all good little words of praise and encouragement, and all quaint pet names and endearments; and I charge said parents to use them justly, but generously, as the deeds of their children shall require.

Item: I leave to children inclusively, but only for the term of their childhood, all and every the flowers of the fields and the blossoms of the woods, with the right to play among them freely according to the customs of children, warning them at the same time against thistles and thorns. And I devise to children the banks of the brooks and the golden sands beneath the waters thereof, and the odors of the willows that dip therein, and the white clouds that float high over the giant trees. And I leave the children the long, long days to be merry in, in a thousand ways, and the night and the trail of the Milky Way to wonder at, but subject nevertheless, to the rights hereinafter given to lovers.

Item: I devise to boys, jointly, all the useful idle fields and commons where ball may be played, all pleasant waters where one may swim, all snowclad hills where one may coast, and all streams and ponds where one may fish, or where, when grim Winter comes, one may skate, to hold the same for the period of their boyhood. And all meadows, with the cloverblossoms and butterflies thereof; the woods with their appurtenances; the squirrels and the birds and echoes and strange noises, and all distant places, which may be visited, together with the adventures there found. And I give to said boys each his own place at the fireside at night, with all pictures that may be seen in the burning wood, and to enjoy without let or hindrance or without any encumbrance or care.

Item: To lovers, I devise their imaginary world, with whatever they may need, as the stars of the sky, the red roses by the wall, the bloom of the hawthorn, the sweet strains of music, and aught else they may desire to figure to each other the lastingness and beauty of their love.

Item: To young men, jointly, I devise and bequeath all the boisterous, inspiring sports of rivalry, and I give to them the disdain of weakness and undaunted confidence in their own strength. Though they are rude, I leave to them the power to make lasting friendships, and of possessing companions, and to them, exclusively, I give all merry songs and grave choruses to sing with lusty voices.

Item: And to those who are no longer children or youths or lovers, I leave memory; and bequeath to them the volumes of the poems of Burns and Shakespeare and of other poets, if there be others, to the end that they may live the old days over again, freely and fully without title or diminution.

Item: To our loved ones with snowy crowns, I bequeath the happpiness of old age, the love and gratitude of their children until they fall asleep.

At the bottom of this will, someone had written, "After all, was he so poor and insane? If that was the world in which he lived, was he not richer than are some who go about freely and who have money in the bank? At any rate, to each of us he bequeathed something. Let us not fail to get our legacy."

Emerson said, "A beautiful behavior is better than a beautiful form; it gives a higher pleasure than statues and pictures; it is the finest of the fine arts."

A father and mother should regularly spend some time alone with each son or daughter. The other night, our young son Paul was in bed. He had not quite settled into sleep. I went into his room, caressed his cheek, and pushed his hair back. I said to him, "Paul, I truly, honestly love you with all my heart. I am so grateful that our Heavenly Father has sent you to our home. No father could be more grateful for a son than we are for you." Then I kissed him goodnight. Would you like to guess what influence that brief experience may have on him? It is my understanding that psychologists believe there is much more, perhaps ten times more, effect from what you say if you are touching a person when you talk to him. This principle should be used with propriety and discretion. Within the family, sweet words carry the greatest impact when accompanied by a touch.

Conversely, it is interesting, as Samuel Smiles states, that "The impolite, impulsive man will . . . sometimes rather lose his friend than his joke. He may surely be pronounced a very foolish person who secures another's hatred at the price of a moment's gratification. It was a saying of Burnel, the engineer—himself one of the kindest-natured of men—that spite and ill-nature are among the most expensive luxuries in life. Dr. Johnson once said: 'Sir, a man has no more right to say a rude thing to another than to knock him down.'" (Smiles, p. 527.)

We find men of influence can be described in these equally beautiful principles also taught by Samuel Smiles:

> The perfection of manner is ease—that it attracts no man's notice as such, but is natural and unaffected. Artifice is incompatible with courteous frankness of manner. Rochefoucauld has said that "nothing so much prevents our being natural as the desire of appearing so." Thus we come round again to sincerity and truthfulness, which find their outward expression in graciousness, urbanity, kindliness and consideration for the feelings of others. The frank and cordial man sets those about him at their ease. He warms and elevates them by his presence, and wins all hearts. Thus, manner, in its highest form, like character, becomes a genuine motive power.
>
> "The love and admiration," says Canon Kingsley, "which that truly brave and loving man, Sir Sidney Smith won from every one, rich and poor, with whom he came in contact, seems to have arisen from the one fact that, without, perhaps, having any such conscious intention, he treated rich and poor, his own servants and the noblemen his guests, alike courteously, considerately, cheerfully, affectionately—so leaving a blessing, and reaping a blessing wherever he went."
>
> Men who toil with their hands, equally with those who do not, may respect themselves and respect one another; and it is by their demeanor to each other—in other words, by their manners—that self-respect as well as

mutual respect are indicated. There is scarcely a moment
in their lives the enjoyment of which might not be en-
hanced by kindliness of this sort—in the workshop, in the
street, or at home. The civil workman will exercise increased power among his class, and gradually induce
them to imitate him by his persistent steadiness, civility
and kindness. One may be polite and gentle with very
little money in his purse. Politeness goes far, yet costs
nothing.

It is the cheapest of all commodities. It is the humblest
of the fine arts, yet it is so useful and pleasure-giving that
it might almost be ranked among the humanities. (Ibid.,
pp. 528-29.)

Those who have the greatest influence on us are those
who have our interest at heart. It has been my custom for
nearly thirty years now to constantly read from the book
Les Miserables, by Victor Hugo. This book has influenced
my life to the point where I have made many commitments to change and be more Christ-like.

In *Les Miserables,* Jean Valjean had promised Cosette's
mother, Fantine, who has died, that he would retrieve
Cosette from the vile people who were supposed to be
caring for her. The Thenardiers treat Cosette worse than
they would treat a stray mongrel. Cosette does all the er-
rands. She does not rank with the Thenardiers' lovely
daughters. Jean Valjean arrives on the scene. He quickly
notices the contempt and disgust that the Thenardiers
have for Cosette. She has no toys and no time to play, and
she is constantly under the evil scrutiny of the Thenardiers.

It is Christmas Eve. Jean Valjean goes out into the
street, buys a beautiful doll, and returns to the inn to give
the doll to Cosette. He asks the Thenardiers for permission. They say yes, but here is the description of how they
felt: "This stranger, this unknown man, who seemed like a
visit from Providence to Cosette, was at the moment the

being which the Thenardiers hated more than aught else in the world." (Hugo, p. 347.)

Finally, everyone goes to bed. Jean Valjean has been shown to his room and left alone.

> The traveller had put his staff and bundle in a corner. The host gone, he sat down in an arm-chair, and remained some time thinking. Then he drew off his shoes, took one of the candles, blew out the other, pushed open the door, and went out of the room, looking about him as if he were searching for something. He passed through a hall, and came to the stairway. There he heard a very soft little sound, which resembled the breathing of a child. Guided by this sound he came to a sort of triangular nook built under the stairs, or, rather, formed by the staircase itself. This hole was nothing but the space beneath the stairs. There, among all sorts of old baskets and old rubbish, in the dust and among the cobwebs, there was a bed; if a mattress so full of holes as to show the straw, and a covering so full of holes as to show the mattress, can be called a bed. There were no sheets. This was placed on the floor immmediately on the tiles. In this bed Cosette was sleeping.
>
> The man approached and looked at her.
>
> Cosette was sleeping soundly; she was dressed. In the winter she did not undress on account of the cold. She held the doll clasped in her arms; its large open eyes shone in the obscurity. From time to time she heaved a deep sigh, as if she were about to wake, and she hugged the doll almost convulsively. There was only one of her wooden shoes at the side of her bed. An open door near Cosette's nook disclosed a large dark room. The stranger entered. At the further end, through a glass window, he perceived two little beds with very white spreads. They were those of Azelma and Eponine. Half hid behind these was a willow cradle without curtains, in which the little boy who had cried all the evening was sleeping.
>
> The stranger conjectured that this room communicated with that of the Thenardiers. He was about to withdraw when his eye fell upon the fireplace, one of those huge tavern fireplaces where there is always so little fire, when there is a fire, and which are so cold to look upon.

In this one there was no fire, there were not even any ashes. What there was, however, attracted the traveller's attention. It was two little children's shoes, of coquettish shape and of different sizes. The traveller remembered the graceful and immemorial custom of children putting their shoes in the fireplace on Christmas night, to wait there in the darkness in expectation of some shining gift from their good fairy. Eponine and Azelma had taken good care not to forget this, and each had put one of her shoes in the fireplace.

The traveller bent over them.

The fairy—that is to say, the mother—had already made her visit, and shining in each shoe was a beautiful new ten-sous piece.

The man rose up and was on the point of going away, when he perceived further along, by itself, in the darkest corner of the fireplace, another object. He looked, and recognised a shoe, a horrid wooden shoe of the clumsiest sort, half broken and covered with ashes and dried mud. It was Cosette's shoe. Cosette, with that touching confidence of childhood which can always be deceived without ever being discouraged, had also placed her shoe in the fireplace.

What a sublime and sweet thing is hope in a child who has never known anything but despair!

There was nothing in this wooden shoe.

The stranger fumbled in his waistcoat, bent over, and dropped into Cosette's shoe a gold Louis.

Then he went back to his room with stealthy tread. (Ibid., pp. 350-51.)

On Christmas Day, Jean Valjean was able to secure Cosette and take her away from this household of vipers. She was only eight, and as she left the Thenardiers behind, she "walked seriously along, opening her large eyes, and looking at the sky. She had put her louis in the pocket of her new apron. From time to time she bent over and cast a glance at it, and then looked at the goodman. She felt somewhat as if she were near God." (Ibid., p. 357.)

How often good, kind, loving people make us feel nearer to God. How great shall be the influence of any true disciple of Christ.

President David O. McKay said, "There is no greater responsibility in the world than the training of a human soul." This training can take many forms.

A bishop once told me of a young man at a missionary preparation workshop. He lazed on the grass a few feet away from the rest of the group. He would occasionally laugh or make fun of the speakers. He would not participate, as he had no intention of serving a mission. Around a campfire that night, during a testimony meeting, this young man stood up and began to talk. He said, "This morning I did not participate in the missionary preparation workshops, but I was listening, I was listening. I have been thinking, thinking a lot." Then, with great emotion he said, "I have made a decision to go on a mission."

In 1982 at Flagstaff, Arizona, a special banquet for Eagle Scouts was held. Attending were 1,150 Eagle Scouts. John Warnick, the director of Mormon relationships for the Scouts, invited all those who would commit to go on a mission to stand. All 1,150 stood.

Later, one of the young men, a Catholic, went to a bishop and said, "I am not a Mormon and I committed to go on a mission. What do I need to do?" The bishop said, "Let's talk to your parents." During the visit with the family, it was decided that the family should hear the missionary discussions. The family, including the Eagle Scout, are now all members of the Church.

Some years back a Scout named Terry was at a Scout camp. That night a full moon hung overhead. The Scoutmaster took Terry by the arm and said, "Let's go for a walk." They went several hundred feet from the cabins. The Scoutmaster said, "Terry, let's kneel here and have a prayer." They knelt together and prayed. After the prayer, Terry's Scoutmaster said to him, "Terry, do you pray?" Terry answered that he did not. "Terry, will you commit to pray every day all the rest of your life?" the Scoutmaster asked. Terry said, "I have never made a commitment unless I intended to keep it." He thought about prayer and decided it was right. It was a good thing. He said to his Scoutmaster, "Yes, I will pray all the rest of my life."

Terry went on to high school, then quarterbacked for the University of Utah, where he was all-conference. He went on to play for the Pittsburgh Steelers. He later said, "I have kept that commitment and I have prayed every morning and night throughout the years."

One of the most Christ-like acts any leader can perform is to go out after the sheep. President Lee once said, "One's love is determined by how much he gives, not how much he gets."

A French scientist, René de Chardan, said, "Some day after we have mastered the winds and the waves, the tides and gravity, we will harness for God the energies of love, and then for the second time in the history of the world man will have discovered fire." Such is the love of a great man in my life, Bruford Reynolds.

As a boy of eleven I used to go over to the old Richards Ward every Tuesday night. The Scouts would be having their Scout meeting. I would lie on the ground and watch through the basement window. The Scouts would have patrol contests, practice using flint and steel, learn first aid, drill, and play games. I could hardly wait to become a Scout.

When I was ordained a deacon I also registered in Scouting. The Scoutmaster, Bruford Reynolds, was also the deacons quorum adviser for a period of time.

Two months after I joined the troop I went to the

Scoutmaster's home to pass off the requirements to become a Second-class Scout. After I had done this, Bruford Reynolds said to me, "Vaughn, you have a lot of leadership ability but we cannot use you because you are rowdy in troop meeting. When you get squared away, we need you."

Having come from a large inactive family that was poor, I had little personal attention. My father had never told me that I could be anything. I gave a great deal of thought to my conduct. I decided to change. The following Tuesday I hardly moved an eyeball. I was as near perfect as I knew how to be.

Bruford Reynolds was true to his word. I became an assistant patrol leader, a patrol leader, assistant senior patrol leader, then senior patrol leader. He believed in me and had a profound impact on my life.

About five years ago I called Bruford Reynolds on the phone. He was a bishop at the time. I said, "May I be invited to speak at your sacrament meeting sometime in the near future?" He said, "We are not supposed to ask the General Authorities to speak in sacrament meetings." "You aren't," I said. "I am asking you." He then said, "I would love to have you come on Easter." So I prepared a talk on the Savior's life.

When I began to speak I first told the people in his ward what a wonderful man their bishop had been in my life. I told them how I used to go over and lie down on the ground and watch the Scout troop through the window. I shared with them examples of great lessons Bruford Reynolds had taught me. I told them of the influence he had had on my life and how he had told me I had leadership abilities. Then I shared with them how much I loved him. After brief comments about the bishop I then spoke about the Savior.

At the conclusion of my talk, Bishop Reynolds stood.

"We are not supposed to speak after General Authorities," he said, "but I want to share this additional part of the story that Elder Featherstone does not know. During part of the time I was Scoutmaster, I also served as Sea Scout skipper. Both groups met on Tuesday—Scouts at seven-thirty, Sea Scouts at eight. I would get Scout meeting started and then I would leave to go to Lincoln Ward where the Sea Scouts met. At eight-thirty I would return to conclude the last half-hour of Scout meeting. Elder Featherstone was my senior patrol leader, and I would leave him in charge of the troop. He isn't the only one who has lain on the ground and watched through the basement window! I used to do that when I would come back from Lincoln Ward. I wanted to see what was going on.

"One night I had a problem and could not make it back to the Scout troop until just before nine o'clock. I did not stop to look in the window but just hurried down the hall to the Scout room. You can learn a lot about what is going on in a Scout meeting by listening at the door. I listened at the door. Elder Featherstone had called the troop together for a Scoutmaster's Minute. I could hear what was being said.

"All of a sudden I heard footsteps behind me. I looked back, and there were four district commissioners from the Boy Scouts who had come to visit our troop. I wondered what they thought when they saw the Scoutmaster standing outside the Scout room listening at the door. I didn't know what to say, so I put my finger to my lips in a hushing signal, and then I motioned for them to listen at the door. They all leaned over and listened. In a minute one of the men said, 'That boy will be a fine leader out in the world some day.' I said, 'No, one day he will lead in high places in this Church.'"

Two years ago we decided to have a reunion and

honor Bruford Reynolds and other Scoutmasters who led us in Richards Ward between 1940 and 1950. The chapel was completely filled with former Scouts. We had raised money to buy some very nice gifts for them, and using an opaque projector we showed pictures of activities and of Scouts during those years. We made a real fuss over Bruford Reynolds and the other great men.

Then we called for a response. Bruford Reynolds stood up and with great tears dimming his eyes he said, "I think this is the greatest day of my life." As I thought about that statement, I looked out across the group of deacons and Scouts grown tall. It included three men who had been stake presidents, two men who had been mission presidents, several men in stake presidencies, thirty-three men who had been bishops, and one who is a General Authority. Then I thought, "Maybe this is what life is all about—to be able to look back and see the young people you have influenced grow up and become leaders in the kingdom."

A short time after that reunion, young Bruford Reynolds, a son, who was also a bishop, called and said, "Did you know my dad is in the hospital? He has had a serious heart attack." I had not known. I told him that I would like to see him but that I had to catch a plane in a little over an hour. I didn't see how I could get up to the hospital before I had to leave. He then said, "Oh, that's okay. Dad is going to be released tomorrow to return home." I said, "Tell him I love him, and I'll drop in to see him as soon as I get back."

I hung up the phone, thought for only a moment, and decided everything else could wait. I took my briefcase and airplane tickets and drove to the LDS Hospital to see Bruford Reynolds. As I walked through the door, our eyes met. The love between a great man and a boy spanned the years. I went over to him and sat down and we talked. Then I said, "I know you have been administered to, but would you feel all right if I knelt by your bed and offered a prayer?" I knelt down and together we prayed. When I finished, my eyes were filled with tears, as were his. Then I bent down over him and kissed him on the forehead and left.

Bruford Reynolds died an hour later. I was one of his boys saying farewell to a great adviser one last time.

My testimony to you is that as a true disciple of Christ, you can have a greater influence on others and are more important to the Church than you would ever dare to suppose.

8

Leadership

Ln his book *The Men Who Wrought*, Ridgwell Cullum describes a particular character with these words: "His mental digestion was devouring hungrily of that force which had come to make his con-temporaries realize that here was a man of that unusual calibre which must ultimately make him a leader of men in whatever walk of life he chose for the *strenuous* jour-ney." (Cullum, p. 21; italics added.)

The course of leadership is a strenuous journey. Some men and women seem to be endowed with character traits that lift them to a position where their influence reaches out in ever-widening circles. The leader is a leader because those with whom he associates, works, plays, or resides are willing to follow.

The God of heaven has endowed each of us with in-comprehensible potential. Each person has the seeds of a divine parentage planted within. We can influence condi-tions and effect changes. Any discussion of leadership must of necessity be limited, for there are a thousand qualities of leadership, and they are as varied as the lead-ers who have them. This chapter will focus on the leader-ship skills that will carry us through the final hours of preparation into the Millennium.

This generation may well require the greatest leader-ship skills, collectively, of any generation. Satan has never been so blatant, so open, so evil. His influence reaches into every dark crevice, every silent recess of the mind. His army is legion. His ranks grow rapidly. He has influence in business, politics, churches, and neighborhoods. His evil is as the Lord declared it would become: a desolating scourge. He is Godless and ruthless; his banners are black; an evil, dark cloud enshrouds his army. His aim is destruction, desolation, murder, rape, robbery, hate, and lust. Who will stand in this gloomy period of the world? Who will engage the foe in battle? Much of it will be hand-to-hand combat. A large measure of it will be mind against mind, spirit against body. Whence cometh deliverance? The gentle God-fearing Saints increase a few here and a few there. Satanic forces increase a hundredfold. But we fear not, for we have the Lord as our leader, and he says, "Let my army become very great, and let it be sanctified before me, that it may become fair as the sun, and clear as the moon, and that her banners may be terrible unto all nations; that the kingdom of this world may be constrained to acknowledge that the kingdom of Zion is in very deed the kingdom of our God and his Christ; therefore, let us become subject unto her laws." (D&C 105:31-32.)

The Lord's army will be fair as the sun, clear as the moon, with terrible banners. Who will prepare this army and all of its leaders? We must, and we will.

Read the words of Heber C. Kimball:

> We think we are secure here in the chambers of the everlasting hills, where we can close those few doors of the canyons against mobs and persecutors, the wicked and the vile, who have always beset us with violence and robbery, but I want to say to you, my brethren, the time is coming when we will be mixed up in these now peaceful valleys to the extent that it will be difficult to tell the face of a Saint from the face of an enemy to the people of God.

> Then, brethren, look out for the great sieve, for there will
> be a great sifting time, and many will fall; for I say unto
> you there is a *test*, a TEST, a TEST coming, and who will be
> able to stand? (Whitney, pp. 445-46.)

He said to beware of the great sieve, for there will come a great sifting time. This leads to the first leadership quality I would like to discuss, the necessity of a deep, abiding testimony.

The enemies of the Church are myriad. They sow the seeds of apostasy. What value is a leader without a testimony? His effort will sway as reeds in the wind. He will lack commitment, influence, inspiration, and the power to motivate. There will be no courage of conviction, no giving of the last ounce of strength for the cause. There will be no battling on when all seems hopeless. To lead in the kingdom, one must have a testimony, strong and bright and true. I have often said that you can line up the intellectuals, the religionists, and the adversaries of the Church, including apostates, from San Francisco to Salt Lake City, four abreast, and have them come at me all day long and tell me that the Church is not true, and when the last man passes by I will still know with everything in my heart and soul that The Church of Jesus Christ of Latter-day Saints is the only authorized and true church on the earth. I may not be able to argue or debate with the intellectuals, but they can never convince or persuade me that my testimony is not true. This kind of testimony puts heart into the leader. It creates righteous fierceness, boldness, and an unconquerable spirit.

Testimony is essential. Heber C. Kimball said, "If you have not got the testimony, live right and call upon the Lord and cease not till you obtain it." The leader with a testimony must feel in his heart and soul a constant desire to build testimony in others. He also said, "The time will

come when no man nor woman will be able to endure on
borrowed light. Each will have to be guided by the light
within himself." (Ibid., p. 450.) The leader must infuse in
those he leads a testimony of fire that does not burn low
when the winds and storms come.

The prophet Ammon gives us insight as to how our
testimonies influence and bring to refuge the souls that
receive their own testimonies:

> Behold, the field was ripe, and blessed are ye, for ye
> did thrust in the sickle, and did reap with your might, yea,
> all day long did ye labor; and behold the number of your
> sheaves! And they shall be gathered into the garners, that
> they are not wasted.
>
> Yea, they shall not be beaten down by the storm at the
> last day; yea, neither shall they be harrowed up by the
> whirlwinds; but when the storm cometh they shall be
> gathered together in their place, that the storm cannot
> penetrate to them; yea, neither shall they be driven with
> fierce winds whithersoever the enemy listeth to carry
> them.
>
> But behold, they are in the hands of the Lord of the
> harvest, and they are his; and he will raise them up at the
> last day.
>
> Blessed be the name of our God; let us sing to his
> praise, yea, let us give thanks to his holy name, for he doth
> work righteousness forever . . .
>
> Behold, how many thousands of our brethren has he
> loosed from the pains of hell; and they are brought to sing
> redeeming love, and this because of the power of his
> word which is in us, therefore have we not great reason to
> rejoice? . . .
>
> Yea, they were encircled about with everlasting dark-
> ness and destruction; but behold, he has brought them
> into his everlasting light, yea, into everlasting salvation;
> and they are encircled about with the matchless bounty of
> his love; yea, and we have been instruments in his hands
> of doing this great and marvelous work. (Alma 26: 5-8, 13,
> 15.)

And then in verse 22 Ammon gives us a vision of what
a leader with a testimony can accomplish:

> He that repenteth and exerciseth faith, and bringeth forth good works, and prayeth continually without ceasing—unto such it is given to know the mysteries of God; yea, unto such it shall be given to reveal things which never have been revealed; yea, and it shall be given unto such to bring thousands of souls to repentance, even as it has been given unto us to bring these our brethren to repentance.

I believe that faith in Christ is the supreme motivator and that testimony is a great, critical element of the Christian leader.

The second trait necessary in the leader is an indomitable will and sense of duty. The sense of duty gives the leader his charge and the indomitable will gives him the tenacity and the perseverance to complete the assignment or to get the results expected.

Plato said, "Let men of all ranks, whether they are successful or unsuccessful, whether they triumph or not—let them do their duty, and rest satisfied." (Smiles, p. 496.)

Another example of duty and will coming together was in the life of George Washington.

> As might be expected of the great Washington, the chief motive power in his life was the spirit of duty. It was the regal and commanding element in his character which gave it unity, compactness and vigor. When he clearly saw his duty before him, he did it at all hazards, and with inflexible integrity. He did not do it for effect, nor did he think of glory, or of fame and its rewards; but of the right thing to be done, and the best way of doing it.
>
> Yet Washington had a most modest opinion of himself; and when offered the chief command of the American patriot army, he hesitated to accept it until it was pressed upon him. When acknowledging in Congress the honor which had been done him in selecting him to so important a trust, on the execution of which the future of his country in a great measure depended, Washington said: "I beg it may be remembered, lest some unlucky event should happen unfavorable to my reputation, that I this

day declare, with the utmost sincerity, I do not think myself equal to the command I am honored with." And in his
letter to his wife, communicating to her his appointment
as commander-in-chief, he said, "I have used every endeavor in my power to avoid it, not only from my un-
willingness to part with you and the family, but from the
consciousness of its being a trust too great for my capacity,
and that I should enjoy more real happiness in one month
with you at home than I have the most distant prospect of
finding abroad, if my stay were to be seven times seven
years. But, as it has been a kind of destiny that has thrown
me upon this service, I shall hope that my undertaking it
is designed for some good purpose. It was utterly out of
my power to refuse the appointment, without exposing
my character to such censures as would have reflected
dishonor upon myself, and given pain to my friends. This,
I am sure, could not and ought not to be pleasing to you,
and must have lessened me considerably in my own
esteem."

Washington pursued his upright course through life,
first as commander-in-chief, and afterwards as president,
never faltering in the path of duty. He had no regard for
popularity, but held to his purpose through good and
through evil report, often at the risk of his power and influence. Thus, on one occasion, when the ratification of a
treaty, arranged by Mr. Jay with Great Britain, was in question, Washington was urged to reject it. But his honor, and
the honor of his country, was committed, and he refused
to do so. A great outcry was raised against the treaty, and
for a time Washington was so unpopular that he is said to
have been actually stoned by the mob. But he nevertheless held it to be his duty to ratify the treaty; and it was
carried out in despite of petitions and remonstrances
from all quarters. "While I feel," he said in answer to the
remonstrance, "the most lively gratitude for the many in-
stances of approbation from my country, I can not other-
wise deserve it than by obeying the dictates of my conscience." (Ibid., p. 500.)

A noted woman, Mrs. Hutchinson, said of her husband
that he was a thoroughly truthful and reliable man: "He
never professed the thing he intended not, nor promised

what he believed out of his power, nor failed in the per-
formance of anything that was in his power to fulfill."
(Ibid., p. 500.)

One last word about will as it relates to duty: "When
Blucher was hastening with his army over bad roads to
the help of Wellington, on the 18th of June 1815, he en-
couraged his troops by words and gestures. 'Forward,
children—forward!' 'It is impossible; it can't be done,' was
the answer. Again and again he urged them. 'Children, we
must get on; you may say it can't be done, but it must be
done! I have promised my brother Wellington—promised, do you hear? You wouldn't have me break my word!'
And it was done." (Ibid., pp. 501-2.)

The third qualification for the leader in God's work is
compassion. This includes love, care, and concern. I listened to a talk by President Heber J. Grant recently and
was so impressed by an example of compassion he used
that I would like to share it here:

> Never did Brother [John] Taylor make a mistake in di-
> recting the course of the Apostles, and neither did
> Brother Woodruff nor Brother Snow nor Brother Joseph
> F. Smith. God, to my knowledge, inspired those men and
> directed them. Brother [Francis M.] Lyman and John
> Henry Smith were told by John Taylor to go to some
> town—I won't mention where it is—and to have a man
> sustained as the president of the stake. Undoubtedly,
> there will be some of you men that know where it was, I
> won't tell it. But Brother Lyman said, "Why, Brother
> Taylor, I know that brother and I know that the people
> will not sustain him." Brother Taylor said, "You and John
> Henry Smith are called upon a mission to have him voted
> for and sustained as president." Brother Lyman, later in
> the day, said, "Suppose these people won't sustain that
> man. What are we to do?" "Yes, but you're called on a mis-
> sion to have him sustained: that is what you're to do." He
> brought it back again, for the third time, and Brother
> Taylor said, "Do you understand English? Don't you know

what mission is placed upon you two men, that is to have
him sustained?" Later in the day, Brother John Henry
thought the president hadn't thoroughly considered the
matter, and he brought it up. He said, "Well, didn't you
hear what I said to Lyman? You two men are called to go
to that place and have the people of that stake sustain this
man."

As we got to the president's office after our meeting in
the Endowment House, [Brother John Henry Smith] said,
"Heber, President Taylor doesn't understand the condition. Those people have rebelled, and they will not sustain this man. He was busy with our regular meeting, and
he didn't get it in his head that it can't be done." I said, "I'll
wait for you." I felt he wouldn't be long. He came out in a
minute, and he said, "I wish to the Lord I hadn't gone in.
Heber, pray for us. Fast and pray for us. I don't see how
under the heavens we can change this condition. Every
bishop and his counselors and the high council and the
patriarch and the presidency of the high priest quorum
have all requested that this good brother be dropped and
that they have another president." And Brother Lyman
said, "John and I will have to pray all the way from Milford
till we get to the place."

When they arrived, Brother Lyman had all these people
together that had signed, and he said, "Now, brethren, we
don't want this man to pitch in to the president and that
man and the other, but we'll step out of the room and you
let one man be appointed to do the talking, and you tell
him everything that you can think of against the president
from start to finish. And if he has forgotten anything, give
him a chance to talk again. Then we'll come back and hear
it all. We're down here to clear up things, and we're going
to do just what you people want us to do." When they got
in the other room, John Henry said, "For heaven's sake,
Lyman, did you lose your head? They want a new president. They've signed their name for a new president."
Lyman said, "Well, it must have been a slip of the tongue."

Well, when the man got through with his talk, which
was nearly an hour, Brother Lyman said, "Has he forgotten anything?" They said, "No, he has told the truth." He
said, "Well, then, it's marvelous. We never dreamed this
man had so many faults and failings. Really, if there is
somebody who would like to tell something good about

him, we'd like to hear it about him." A man got up, and he said, "I can say something good about him, about his generosity and his liberality and his good life." Then he commenced weeping and said, "Brother Lyman, please scratch my name off the list and let me vote for that man tomorrow." Brother Lyman said, "All right, anybody else feel that way?" About one third of them got up, and he said, "Well, you go home then. It is pretty late and the other two-thirds of us will discuss this matter." It took over an hour for them to tell this story. He said, "Now, get up and tell that story over again because it's news to us. We never dreamed the brother had so many failings." And the man got up and told it over again. Another man jumped up and said, "Brother Lyman, please take my name off the list." Brother Lyman said, "All right, anybody else feel that way?"

About half of them stood up. He said, "All right, you folks are wondering why you're out so late; we'll excuse you. Now," he said, "get up and tell us that story again." The man stood up and told the story again. Brother Lyman said, "Two men have tried to tell some good about this man and failed and have asked permission to vote for him tomorrow. Anybody else here that feels to sustain him?" And they all stood up. He said, "All right, good brethren," and he turned to John Henry and said, "John, will you sustain him?" John laughed and said, "I will." By this time I believe it was about half past twelve or one in the morning.

The next morning Brother Lyman was able to say to the people, "All of the bishops and their counselors, and the high council, and the patriarch, and the high priest quorum, every one of them have asked for permission to vote for Brother so-and-so as the president of your stake. We've agreed to let them. If any of you want to vote the other way, there will be no condemnation." They got a unanimous vote to sustain that man as president. When they returned, Brother Taylor said, "It wasn't such a hard job after all, was it?"

"Now," he said, "Brother Lyman, the brother is a big-hearted, fine man, but he makes mistakes. With that large arm of yours, put it around him—go down in three months—he's sick abed now. He would have died broken-hearted if he hadn't been sustained. He'll be well in three months, feeling fine. Go down, put your arm around him, and say, 'Now that the people are loving you and have unanimously sustained you, don't you think it would be wise to resign?' And he'll jump at the chance, and you assume the authority to accept his resignation." And that is how it worked out.

There are things I could go on by the hour telling you that Brother Taylor's advice was followed, and I want to tell you, starting with Brigham Young and coming down to your humble servant, the Lord has been with us and has directed us. May the Lord help us to so live that you will sustain us. (*Voices of the Prophets,* cassette 2, side 2.)

President Taylor had great compassion for this brother, and compassion is an essential trait of the leader who would emulate the Master.

The fourth trait is one that is often overlooked. One must have a lightness of heart, a buoyant spirit, a sense of cheerfulness, a sense of humor.

Elder John Sonnenberg, a regional representative, told a story of when he was a young father. He and his wife had seven children and only one car. He would take the car to work, and if Sister Sonnenberg wanted to go somewhere, she would have to take the bus. One day, Sister Sonnenberg and all seven children waited at the bus stop. The bus came along, and Sister Sonnenberg climbed on and put in her token. Then she put in a token for each of her children. The bus driver, amazed, said, "Lady, are these all your children or is this a picnic?" She said, "They are all my children and it's no picnic."

We've got to be careful not to take ourselves too seriously. Put good, honest, appropriate humor and fun into life. The leader who cares about people and loves them will always try to have a positive mental attitude with a seasoned sense of humor. He will put fun into his work so that it does not become a drudgery.

The next leadership trait is mental and physical ambition. Leadership, for the disciple of Christ, takes serious thinking. There is no harder work than thinking. A leader has to think through all of the negative aspects of the work to be done or duty to be filled and to overcome the obstacles. He needs to be able to think of ingenious ways to train and teach.

Years ago, while I was in the grocery business, I came across a series of leadership booklets published by the Dartnell Corporation. I received one booklet each month on a different dimension of leadership. Following is an excerpt from one booklet that shows a leader who used his imagination to train employees in a dramatic way:

> The trainees were clustered around the supervisor when disaster struck. Frozen with panic, unable to move, they watched in horrified fascination as the machine inexorably devoured the tie, pulling the supervisor forward into the perilous zone. They heard the whine of the machine, the gears single-mindedly meshing. Then, at the last moment, the supervisor pushed the release button and pulled out a ragged tie.
>
> No trainee ever forgot how quickly, how easily long hair or loose clothing could be caught in the maws of that dangerous machine. Only much later they discovered that was how the supervisor rid himself of his unwanted Christmas ties. It was an especially memorable lesson, because their attention was emotionally heightened by the staging of this particular demonstration. (Wells, p. 16.)

The creative thinking of a leader is necessary and may be needed to save a life and teach safety, or it may be to motivate, to instruct, to teach, to respond with well-thought-out answers. The leader will avoid doubts, falterings, and other fears by being mentally prepared.

The use of our mental capacity does not include unrighteous dominion or intimidation. Thomas Jefferson said, "I have sworn upon the altar of God eternal hostility against every form of tyranny over the mind of man." (National Park Service pamphlet, reprint 1973.)

He also said:

> Almighty God hath created the mind free. All attempts to influence it by temporal punishments or burdens . . . are a departure from the plan of the Holy Author of our religion. . . . No man shall be compelled to frequent or support any religious worship or ministry or shall otherwise suffer on account of his religious opinions or belief, but all men shall be free to profess and by argument to maintain, their opinions in matters of religion. I know but one code of morality for men whether acting singly or collectively. (Ibid.)

Yes, we must use our minds and our mental ambition to bless people. We must expand our appetite for knowledge. In *Les Miserables,* Victor Hugo states:

> Intellectual and moral growth is not less indispensable than material amelioration. Knowledge is a viaticum, thought is of primary necessity, truth is nourishment as well as wheat. A reason, by fasting from knowledge and wisdom, becomes puny. Let us lament as over stomachs, over minds who do not eat. If there is anything more poignant than a body agonising for want of bread, it is a soul which is dying of hunger for light. (Hugo, p. 842.)

In addition to mental ambition, our physical capacity is critical. Sometimes the leader must simply go to work. At a recent zone conference for missionaries, I walked into the cultural hall where so many missionaries had been served a fine lunch. I was startled to see the custodian, a woman, putting away all the tables and chairs. Eighty missionaries were standing around talking while this good sister cleaned up after them. I immediately took off my coat, took the woman over and sat her down, or rather attempted to, and then started putting up the chairs and tables. A General Authority has a fairly high profile, and soon many missionaries were assisting me in the task. Sometimes there is no substitute for the leader simply getting into the middle of the work.

Sir William Osler, great Canadian physician and professor of medicine, whose book *The Principles and Practices of Medicine* is still used as a textbook after eighty-two years, believed work to be the master word in life. He wrote, "It is the touchstone of progress, the measure of success, and the fount of hope. It is directly responsible for all advances in medicine and technology." (*Royal Bank of Canada Newsletter*, vol. 55, no. 9.)

On the other end of the spectrum is what is referred to as the "Gooch letter":

> The newly hired traveling salesman wrote his first sales report to the home office. It stunned the brass in the sales department.
>
> "I seen this outfit which they ain't never bot a dimes worth of nothing from us and I sole them a coupl hunred thosand dollars of guds. I am now goin to Chicawgo."
>
> But before the illiterate itinerant could be given the "heave-ho" by the sales manager, along came another letter:
>
> "I cum hear and sole them haff a millyun."
>
> Fearful that it might be true and fearful at the same time of his company's image if he didn't fire the illiterate peddler, the sales manager decided to dump the problem in the lap of the president. The following morning, the members in the ivory tower of the sales department were flabbergasted to see the two letters from the new traveling salesman posted on the bulletin board and this letter from the president:
>
> "We ben spending too much time tryin two spel instead of tryin to sel. Lets wach thoes sails. I want everyboddy shuld reed these letters from Gooch who is on the rode doing a grate job, and you shuld go out and do like he done."
>
> Moral: Too many people are not result oriented—they are appearance oriented and allow their personal hangups to interfere with progress.

So often we see missionaries who come from a farm or a community where survival is more essential than education. There young men oftentimes know how to work but they destroy the English language or spell abominably. However, because of their purity, their love for people, and their ability to work, they baptize many people, sometimes far more than those who speak impeccable English and spell accurately but have never learned to work.

The disciple of Christ will be a worker. As we read the scriptures we are impressed with the number of times Jesus spent much of the night in meditation, prayer, and pondering. Equally as impressive was his example of working physically, so much so that he slept while the tempest raged. Think of the physical and mental agony suffered in Gethsemane's garden. There was not one other soul that could have suffered so exquisitely and bear the burden that he bore. A leader would do well to remind himself that the Lord's counsel for us to serve with heart, might, mind, and strength unites physical and mental ambition into a vital leadership dimension.

The final leadership trait is the ability to motivate others. I have just completed reading *Les Miserables* by Victor Hugo for the fourth time. It is the complete, unabridged volume of 1,222 pages. I have asked myself several times why I have been motivated to read that volume again when there are so many books I have never read that I ought to read. I finally determined that my experiences with the book in the past were so pleasurable and fulfilling, so exciting and motivating, so inspiring and spiritual, that I felt a great need and urge to repeat them. Isn't motivation like that? We do not have a difficult time motivating someone to do something that brings them great pleasure or satisfaction. One of the great keys in motivating others, then, is to turn every necessary work into a fulfilling experience.

Faith in Christ is the greatest motivator of all. But other motivators are also important. Sometimes motivation comes through words in a book by a great leader (anyone who inspires and motivates someone else is a leader). Samuel Smiles wrote:

> Of Condorcet's "Eloge of Haller," Horner said: "I never rise from the account of such men without a sort of thrilling palpitation about me, which I know not whether I should call admiration, ambition or despair." And speaking of the "Discourses" of Sir Joshua Reynolds, he said: "Next to the writings of Bacon, there is no book which has more powerfully impelled me to self-culture. He is one of the first men of genius who has condescended to inform the world of the steps by which greatness is attained. The confidence with which he asserts the omnipotence of human labor has the effect of familiarizing his reader with the idea that genius is an acquisition rather than a gift; whilst with all there is blended so naturally and eloquently the most elevated and passionate admiration of excellence, that upon the whole there is no book of a more inflammatory effect." It is remarkable that Reynolds himself attributed his first passionate impulse towards the study of art, to reading Richardson's account of a great painter; and Hayden was in like manner afterwards inflamed to follow the same pursuit by reading of the career of Reynolds. Thus the brave and inspiring life of one man lights a flame in the minds of others of like faculties and impulse: and where there is equally vigorous effort, like distinction and success will almost surely follow. Thus the chain of example is carried down through time in an endless succession of links—admiration exciting imitation, and perpetuating the true aristocracy of genius. (Smiles, pp. 597-98.)

Motivation may also come through the example of a person with a good character. Samuel Smiles says, "Character is human nature in its best form." He also says, "Men of character are not only the conscience of society, but in every well governed state they are its best motive power, for it is moral qualities in the main which rule the world." (Ibid., p. 600.) Character, then, is indeed a trait essential to motivating others.

"Even in war," Napoleon said, "the moral is to the physical as ten to one." (Ibid., pp. 600-601.) Consider the character of Francis Horner, a former member of the British House of Commons:

> "The valuable and peculiar light," says Lord Cockburn, "in which his history is calculated to inspire every right-minded youth, is this. He died at the age of thirty-eight possessed of greater public influence than any other private man, and admired, beloved, trusted, and deplored by all, except the heartless or the base. No greater homage was every paid in Parliament to any deceased member. Now let every young man ask—how was this attained? By rank? He was the son of an Edinburgh merchant. By wealth? Neither he, nor any of his relations, ever had a superfluous sixpence. By office? He held but one, and only for a few years, of no influence, and with very little pay. By talents? His were not splendid, and he had no genius. Cautious and slow, his only ambition was to be right. By eloquence? He spoke in a calm, good taste, without any of the oratory that either terrifies or seduces. By any fascination of manner? His was only correct and agreeable. By what, then, was it? Merely by sense, industry, good principles, and a good heart—qualities which no well-constituted mind need ever despair of attaining. It was the force of his character that raised him; and his character not impressed upon him by nature, but formed, out of no peculiarly fine elements, by himself. There were many in the House of Commons of far greater ability and eloquence. But no one surpassed him in the combination of an adequate portion of these moral [qualities]. Horner was born to show what moderate powers, unaided by any thing whatever except culture and goodness, may achieve, even when these powers are displayed amidst the competition and jealousy of public life. (Ibid., pp. 601-2.)

Oh, the power of motivation in a noble character! Trust is another powerful motivating force. As a mission president, I trusted all the missionaries. Only a very few violated the trust. We all have a basic need to be trusted, for someone to have confidence in us. Being trusted creates a desire to perform, to not let down the leader who trusts. Heavenly Father has given us our agency, trusting that we will exercise it to bring about the exaltation of ourselves and others. There is something noble about trusting someone, and something far more noble in being able to be trusted.

The Lord has taught us much about motivation. He has said:

> The rights of the priesthood are inseparably connected with the powers of heaven, and . . . the powers of heaven cannot be controlled nor handled only upon the principles of righteousness.
>
> That they may be conferred upon us, it is true; but when we undertake to cover our sins, or to gratify our pride, our vain ambition, or to exercise control or dominion or compulsion upon the souls of the children of men, in any degree of unrighteousness, behold, the heavens withdraw themselves; the Spirit of the Lord is grieved; and when it is withdrawn, Amen to the priesthood or the authority of that man. . . .
>
> We have learned by sad experience that it is the nature and disposition of almost all men, as soon as they get a little authority, as they suppose, they will imediately begin to exercise unrighteous dominion. . . .
>
> No power or influence can or ought to be maintained by virtue of the priesthood, only by persuasion, by long-suffering, by gentleness and meekness, and by love unfeigned; by kindness, and pure knowledge, which shall greatly enlarge the soul without hypocrisy, and without guile—reproving betimes with sharpness, when moved upon by the Holy Ghost; and then showing forth afterwards an increase of love toward him whom thou hast reproved, lest he esteem thee to be his enemy; that he may

know that thy faithfulness is stronger than the cords of death.

Let thy bowels also be full of charity towards all men, and to the household of faith, and let virtue garnish thy thoughts unceasingly; then shall thy confidence wax strong in the presence of God; and the doctrine of the priesthood shall distill upon thy soul as the dews from heaven.

The Holy Ghost shall be thy constant companion, and thy scepter an unchanging scepter of righteousness and truth; and thy dominion shall be an everlasting dominion, and without compulsory means it shall flow unto thee forever and ever. (D&C 121:36-37, 39,41-46.)

These are the principles that motivate. There are numerous others that could be included, but let me end this chapter with this touching story that shows a true Christian leader in action:

A Manchester warehouseman published an exeedingly scurrilous pamphlet against the firm of Grant Brothers, holding up the elder partner to ridicule as "Billy Button." William was informed by some one of the nature of the pamphlet, and his observation was that the man would live to repent of it. "Oh!" said the libeller, when informed of the remark, "he thinks that some time or other I shall be in his debt; but I will take good care of that." It happens, however, that men in business do not always foresee who shall be their creditor, and it so turned out that the Grants' libeller became a bankrupt, and could not complete his certificate and begin business again without obtaining their signature. It seemed to him a hopeless case to call upon that firm for any favor, but the pressing claims of his family forced him to make the application. He appeared before the man whom he had ridiculed as "Bill Button" accordingly. He told his tale and produced his certificate. "You wrote a pamphlet against us once?" said Mr. Grant. The supplicant expected to see his document thrown into the fire; instead of which Grant signed the name of the firm, and thus completed the necessary certificate. "We make it a rule," said he, handing it back, "never to refuse signing the certificate of an honest

tradesman, and we have never heard that you were anything else." The tears started into the man's eyes. "Ah,"
continued Mr. Grant, "you see my saying was true, that
you would live to repent writing that pamphlet. I did not
mean it as a threat—I only meant that some day you
would know us better, and repent having tried to injure
us." "I do, I do, indeed, repent it." "Well, well, you know
us now. But how do you get on—what are you going to
do?" The poor man stated that he had friends who would
assist him when his certificate was obtained. "But how are
you off in the meantime?" The answer was, that having
given up every farthing to his creditors, he had been com-
pelled to stint his family in even the common necessaries
of life, that he might be enabled to pay for his certificates.
"My good fellow, this will never do; your wife and family
must not suffer in this way; be kind enough to take this
ten-pound note to your wife from me; there, there, now—
don't cry, it will be all well with you yet; keep up your
spirits, set to work like a man, and you will raise your
head among the best of us." The overpowered man en-
deavored with choking utterances to express his gratitude, but in vain; and putting his hand to his face, he went
out of the room sobbing like a child. (Smiles, pp. 613-14.)

Testimony, an indomitable will and a sense of duty,
compassion, a sense of humor, mental and physical ambition, and the ability to motivate—all these are important
leadership traits of the disciple of Christ.

Bibliography

Cullum, Ridgwell. *The Men Who Wrought.* Philadelphia: George W. Jacobs and Company, 1916.

Dostoyevsky, Fyodor. *The Brothers Karamazov.* New York: The Modern Library, n.d.

Felleman, Hazel, ed. *The Best Loved Poems of the American People.* Garden City, N.Y.: Doubleday and Co., 1936.

Hugo, Victor. *Les Miserables.* Translated by Charles E. Wilbour. New York: The Modern Library, n.d.

Hymns. Rev. and enl. Salt Lake City: The Church of Jesus Christ of Latter-day Saints, 1948.

Jordan, David Starr. *The Strength of Being Clean.* New York and Boston: H. M. Caldwell Co., 1900.

Mandino, Og. *The Greatest Salesman in the World.* New York: Frederick Fell Publishers, 1968.

McGinnis, Alan Loy. "The Whole Person—Myth & Reality." *1982 MDRT Proceedings.*

National Park Service pamphlet on the Thomas Jefferson Memorial, GPO 1973-515-971/73. Washington, D.C.: Department of the Interior, reprint 1973.

Richards, Stephen L. *Where Is Wisdom?* Salt Lake City: Deseret Book Company, 1955.

Smiles, Samuel. *Happy Homes and the Hearts That Make Them.* Chicago: U.S. Publishing House, 1882.

Vital Speeches of the Day. June 1, 1980; January 15, 1981; May 15, 1982; September 15, 1982.

Voices of the Prophets. Cassette Tape. Provo, Utah: BYU Sound, 1978.

Wells, E. F. *What an Executive Should Know about Extras That Build Leadership.* Chicago: The Dartnell Corporation, 1971.

Whitney, Orson F. *Life of Heber C. Kimball.* Salt Lake City: Bookcraft, 1967.

Index